SOUL CARE
Deliverance and Renewal
Through the Christian Life

A
BRIDGEPOINT
BOOK

BridgePoint,
the academic
imprint of
Victor Books, is
your connection
for the best in
serious reading
that integrates
the passion of
the heart with
the scholarship
of the mind.

SOUL CARE

Deliverance

and Renewal

Through the

Christian Life

KENNETH J. COLLINS

A
BRIDGEPOINT
BOOK

D E D I C A T I O N

For Marilyn, Brooke, and Lauren

EG MO

Unless otherwise noted, Scripture quotations are taken from
the *Holy Bible, New International Version*®. Copyright © 1973, 1978, 1984
by International Bible Society.
Used by permission of Zondervan Publishing House. All rights reserved.
Other quotations are from the
New American Standard Bible, © the Lockman Foundation
1960, 1962, 1963, 1968, 1971, 1972, 1973, 1975, 1977.

Editor: Robert N. Hosack
Designer: Andrea Boven

Library of Congress Cataloging-in-Publication Data

Collins, Kenneth J.
  Soul care : deliverance and renewal through the Christian life / Kenneth J. Collins
    p.   cm.
  Includes bibliographical references.
  ISBN: 1-56476-421-4
  1. Christian life. 2. Good and evil. 3. Sin. I. Title.
BV4501.2.C643 1995
248.4 — dc20   95-33110
                                                                     CIP

BridgePoint is the academic imprint of Victor Books.

© 1995 by Victor Books/SP Publications, Inc.
All rights reserved.
Printed in the United States of America.

1   2   3   4   5   6   7   8   9   10   Printing/Year   99   98   97   96   95

For information write
Victor Books,
1825 College Avenue,
Wheaton, Illinois 60187.

CONTENTS

INTRODUCTION 7

1. THE ROOT OF THE PROBLEM 13

2. THE CONSTRUCTION OF THE KINGDOM OF SELF 32

3. THE ENSLAVEMENT OF THE SELF:
Money, Sex, and the Pursuit of Pleasure 56

4. THE SELF THREATENED:
Ambition, Envy, Strife, and Anger 79

5. THE DELUSIONS OF THE SELF:
False Hope and Bad Faith 99

6. THE KINGDOM OF GOD:
The Cross of Christ and the Gift of Faith 120

7. ABIDING IN THE KINGDOM OF GOD:
The Disciplines of the Liberated Life, Part I 147

8. ABIDING IN THE KINGDOM OF GOD:
The Disciplines of the Liberated Life, Part II 168

POSTSCRIPT 185

NOTES 189

INDEX 195

INTRODUCTION

You will know the truth, and the truth will set you free" (John 8:32).

In an age which is greatly taken by the scientific method, in a time when facts seem to take precedence over values, and in a culture where technology outpaces moral deliberation, it is important to consider in a probing way the phenomenon of the destruction of human values, what we otherwise call evil.

Several years ago Karl Menninger wrote his classic work *What Ever Became of Sin?* and asked American culture to consider evil, not simply in terms of secular models, but also in terms of one's relation to God. He suggested, in other words, that perhaps a spiritual dimension was necessary in order to see evil for what it is and in order to overcome it successfully. More recently, M. Scott Peck, the noted psychiatrist and author, published *The People of the Lie* and implored both the psychiatric community and the clergy to reckon with serious and tragic evil, the kind which ensnares a personality and robs it of both peace and joy. Moreover, Peck suggested that the subtlety and mysteriousness of evil may not be revealed at all, except that traditional psychoanalytic analyses be supplemented by spiritual ones.

In the twentieth century, under the weight of naturalism and philosophical materialism, we have tried to believe that a human being is simply a body and is, therefore, utterly amenable to scientific analysis. We have celebrated what can be seen, heard, touched, smelled, or tasted, but we have looked askance at the unseen, at that which can only be discerned through the depths of the human heart. As a consequence, we have, for the most part, discarded the ancient language of the soul and other spiritual terminology (which go back at least to the time of Plato) as useful models to describe the reality of men and women.

Today, however, through the rise of postmodernism, such broad naturalistic beliefs are being called into question by leading philosophers and other serious thinkers, not because these beliefs no longer have any explanatory power, but because an increasing number of people are coming to the conclusion that human beings are far more than these viewpoints can allow. For many, the idea of men and women as living souls, as spiritual beings, must be entertained if we want to grapple with and understand even some of the more mundane forms of good and evil. There is a different mood abroad. According to *Newsweek*, "Now it's suddenly OK, even chic, to use the S words — soul, sacred, spiritual, sin. In a *Newsweek* Poll, a majority of Americans (58 percent) say they feel the need to experience spiritual growth."[1]

Bu' what is authentic spirituality? In light of the above concerns and climate, this work will attempt to fill a contemporary void by taking into account the relational nature of human beings and their grace-assisted capacity for transcendence through an examination of the rich spiritual tradition of the West both in terms of Scripture and also in terms of spiritual classics. Indeed, readers should find the perspective of this literature quite remarkable in many ways for it not only offers a contrast to some modern thinking, but it is also keenly aware of the dynamics of the soul. This canon, for instance, is well apprised of the subtleties of temptation; it is articulate in terms of the operations of the will, and it is knowledgeable with respect to overcoming the dogs of the spirit in terms of alienation, depression, and despair.

To be sure, models — ways of thinking about good and evil — that are centuries old, rich in meaning, and which were used by the Apostle Paul, St. Augustine, St. Teresa, John of the Cross, Martin Luther, John Calvin, John Wesley, and others as they thought through their own moral and spiritual conditions, are still useful and relevant today. Accordingly, the moral and spiritual values of good and evil, seen from a perspective which breaks out of the alienation of the isolated self and calls it into question, warrants further exploration, especially from people who have suffered too long under the narrowness and constraints of naturalistic beliefs.

The book which follows, then, is an invitation to reflect on the values of good and evil, the nature of spirituality, and how appeal to a transcendent dimension is often necessary to overcome some of the more serious forms of human malaise. Accordingly, in the first chapter, we will present various options for reckoning with human evil. Some of the models examined will presuppose naturalism and will, therefore, deny the reality of God, spirit, and soul. For example, the thoughts of Marx and Freud, which are oriented toward the scientific method as their basic paradigm, are adept in terms of their assessment of empirical and factual relationships, but both strain, at times, in presenting a thorough and sophisticated conception of human evil, an evil which is perhaps best defined, at least on a personal level, as a divided will in which the ego is virtually powerless, and as the destruction of human *values*.

In contrast to these contemporary models, some more popular than others, we will explore the perspective of the Bible, as well as that of the church throughout her rich history, in terms of the broader question of "what is wrong with humanity?" What, in other words, lies at the root of human evil? And for those modern readers who strongly identify with North American secular culture and who therefore immediately discount the biblical material, they are, perhaps, in for a surprise. They may find, after all, that the Bible's paradigm or central model for reckoning with human evil, which is alienation and unbelief, is far more sophisticated and has far greater explanatory power than they had imagined. We will demonstrate such sophistication; we will explore such power throughout the book.

Astute readers will soon realize that the work is arranged, at least on one level, in terms of the seven deadly sins which arise from the root of evil presented in the first chapter. To illustrate, chapter 2 explores the construction of the "kingdom of self," a term borrowed from Earl Jabay, which is otherwise known as *pride* and self-love. Moreover, we will indicate why this "self-curvature" makes it impossible for the autonomous self to solve its own problems without an appeal to that which is beyond itself, namely, God. Chapter 3 will then proceed to describe "the enslavement of the self" which flows from unbelief and pride and which is manifested through such things as greed (money), lust (sex), and gluttony (the pursuit of pleasure). Continuing the larger theme of the book, chapter 4, entitled "The Self Threatened," will examine anger and envy as well as strife and ambition as they lay hold of the human personality and rob it of both its integrity and joy. And chapter 5, "The Delusions of the Self," will chronicle many of the vain attempts of the self to solve its own problems, its own evil, apart from the grace of God.

Considering the larger structure of the book, the first five chapters form a unit by themselves and represent a diagnosis of the problem, an analysis of human ills that grows out of my many years of academic training, my considerable counseling with others, and, in part, through my own experience. Moreover, this diagnosis cannot be rushed. Indeed, if we fail to see the problem clearly for what it is, in both candor and honesty (and this may be painful), we will hardly be able to comprehend the appropriate solution later on. These early chapters, then, are very valuable in assisting readers to reflect on their own lives, in a serious and penetrating way, in terms of the question of human evil, the transcending of such evil, and the larger approach toward happiness.

Chapters 6, 7, and 8 constitute the other major structural unit, and they form a contrast to the first five chapters in that they offer a prescription for the problems diagnosed earlier. With chapter 6, for example, we have left the "kingdom of self," to enter "the kingdom of God," a much different kingdom, a kingdom which calls into question and which eventually overthrows some of our earlier, unexamined values. Not surprisingly, the cross of Christ is at the heart of this chapter, and its light is allowed to reflect back on the forms of evil considered earlier. Indeed, the cross sounds the death knell not only for unbelief and pride, but also for the vain attempts (and there are many of them) which the self manufactures, out of pride and a sinful imagination, to right itself with God. Moreover, this chapter will make clear why, after the descent into human evil, a direct approach to God is no longer possible. It will make clear, in other words, why anxiety, fear, and guilt bar the way, and why a mediator is, therefore, necessary.

The last two chapters of the work entitled, "Abiding in the Kingdom of God," consider the personal, corporate, and public disciplines which are necessary in order to maintain a vital spiritual life, to remain in the kingdom of God, and to thrive, spiritually speaking, by receiving the ongoing grace of the One who is beyond us. Such disciplines as reading the Bible, praying, fasting, receiving the Lord's Supper, as well as service and evangelism, are a few of the practices which make up these disciplines. Moreover, the orientation of these disciplines toward God and neighbor make them especially valuable for those men and women who want to partake of the kingdom of God's rich banquet — marked by a menu of larger joys and deeper satisfactions which far surpass the limited offerings of the kingdom of self.

O N E
THE ROOT OF THE PROBLEM

There are a thousand hacking at the branches of evil to one who is striking at the root" (Henry David Thoreau).

Daily newspapers are a good window on the full range of human behavior; they graphically display humanity's highest achievements as well as its worse defeats. They can show, for example, how a local community can come together to save a child trapped in an abandoned well, or they can describe in grisly detail the psychology and actions of a serial killer as he stalks his prey. Again, newspapers can depict international cooperation among scientists to rid the stratosphere of pollution, or they can chronicle the ongoing assault on war-torn Bosnia.

Unfortunately, one does not have to look to the daily newspapers, to international politics, or to famous people for instances of disturbing human evil. It's much closer to home than we think. Perhaps every adult alive in America today has either directly experienced the agony of a significant loss or been quite close to someone else who has. How many homes, for instance, have been ravaged by the tornado of alcoholism or drug addiction? How many children have borne the burden of child abuse painfully, fearfully, and silently? And how many marriages have been torn apart by forces that neither husband nor wife clearly understood, but which left in their wake resentment, anger, crippled emotions, and troubled children? Add to these ills the afflictions of poverty, malnutrition, neglect, rage, jealousy, revenge, selfish ambition, lust, and outright hatred, and an almost baffling and overwhelming picture of human evil emerges. But is there, perhaps, a common thread which ties all of this together? Put another way, is there an essence, an irreducible core, to human evil? Some well-known thinkers, at least, have thought so.

THE PROBLEM ACCORDING TO TWENTIETH-CENTURY THOUGHT

Part of the problem in diagnosing what's wrong with humanity is that the diagnosis itself is often dependent on just what are taken to be the symptoms of the "disease" and on what level of human experience the analysis will focus. Sigmund Freud, for instance, takes the individual personality as his chief point of departure, while Karl Marx and other leftist political thinkers explore the broader dimension of social structures and economic relationships. However, the following views, though they differ in their level of analysis, are all similar in that each affirms, in its own way, that it has discovered the root of the problem and that its critique is, therefore, in a real sense radical.

Karl Marx

If you ask a class of college students to write down on a sheet of paper the names of the three most influential people in the twentieth century, the name of Karl Marx invariably appears. These students have not made a historical or chronological error; they are well aware that Marx died in the nineteenth century. And yet they argue that this German political theorist is very much alive today, even after the collapse of the Soviet Union and its empire, since over a billion people live under governments which continue to look to his thought for guidance. More to the point, what makes Marx's thought still popular today among liberation theologians and the people of third-world countries is his claim that he had found the key to historical processes as well as to many of the ills which plague the human community.

The scope of Marx's analysis is quite broad, a perspective

which he inherited from Hegel. However, unlike the philosophical idealist Hegel, who had argued that reality is essentially Mind or Spirit, Marx taught that reality is basically matter and that it is, therefore, the economic and *material* relationships of society which give rise to everything that shapes a particular culture: its art, philosophy, literature, religion, and science. Accordingly, Marx maintained that the mode of production of a society, that is, how the instruments of production, like factories and raw materials, are controlled, determines the very life and culture of that society and its individual members. For example, in the capitalist mode of production as in the United States, utilities, factories, and raw materials are not in the hands of the state or a central authority, but are privately owned, most often in the hands of corporations. However, in the socialist mode, as in the People's Republic of China, the means of production are not privately owned but are administered by the state on behalf of the workers, the proletariat. The point is, and it's an important one for Marx, these two different economic structures necessarily lead to different cultures.

For Marx, then, the key to the evils of poverty, infant mortality, greed, prostitution, and the like lies not in changing the human heart, but in changing the economic and material forces of a society which give rise to these evils. The solution lies neither in preaching nor in ethical appeals, but rather in economic restructuring. In fact, later Marxists were so optimistic about the benefits of a shift from the capitalist to the socialist mode of production that they believed once they put their economic program in place, they would usher in "the new man." However, recent history in Eastern Europe and the former Soviet Union has shattered such idealism and optimism — perhaps forever.

Sigmund Freud

Another European thinker who attempted to determine the root causes of human ills, but in a much different way, was Sigmund Freud, an Austrian doctor and psychoanalyst. And while we freely acknowledge that much of psychiatry and psychotherapy have moved beyond Freud, especially in terms of psychoanalytic theory, Freud's influence continues. Indeed, Freud looked favorably on the Enlightenment's notion of the autonomous, self-ruled person and mediated this philosophical legacy to his heirs in the social scientific community. More to the point, the Austrian doctor wedded a philosophical position with a psychological one; that is, Freud strongly associated the self as independent and sovereign not with any sort of imbalance or lack of perspective, but with a state of health—an association which is often assumed, though seldom questioned, by many theorists today.

At any rate, for Freud, various neuroses, sexual and otherwise, ultimately grow out of a disruption of the harmonious relationship between the id (loosely identified as the pleasure principle), the ego (reality principle), and the superego (ideal principle, conscience) which make up the personality.[1] Thus, the ego in its attempt to avoid anxiety and in order to mask internal conflict may employ methods known as defense mechanisms which distort reality and which thereby hinder normal psychological development. The defense mechanism of repression, for instance, may force from consciousness a childhood experience of repeated physical abuse in order to protect the personality. Viewed another way, the heart of the problem, the inner conflict between the id, ego, and superego is not allowed to register in the conscious mind because of this repression. Moreover, it is clear from Freud's writings that many of the decisive repressions arise in the early years.

If Freud's diagnosis of human ills is accurate, then a return to well-being consists in the restoration of a harmonious balance between the id, ego, and superego and the individual's larger relationship with the world. This can be accomplished, in part, through the technique of psychoanalysis or what is sometimes called "insight therapy." The patient, with the assistance of a therapist, breaks through the defense mechanisms of the personality in order that the repressed material can be brought into consciousness. And the transfer of this "material" from the unconscious to the conscious mind is aided by free association (Freudian "slips") and by the analysis and interpretation of dreams. But note that healing in this context arises essentially out of insight or through greater self-awareness; knowledge, in other words, is therapeutic; insight is redemptive.

Though many psychoanalysts and theorists like Erikson, S
van, Fairbairn, Jacobson, and Guntrip have since moved beyond
Freud and stress to a greater or lesser degree object relations
theory (interpersonal relationships), some of them continue to
search for the origin of "evil" in early childhood. Guntrip, for
example, is typical of this tendency.

> It becomes apparent that we do not by any means entirely grow
> out of our childhood experiences, and that, in so far as they are a
> source of acute anxiety and insecurity and angers, a great deal of
> all this is buried in the unconscious while our conscious self of
> everyday living develops on either a conformity or a rebellion
> basis. . . . [2]

The problem, however, is that many people today are beginning to question the appeal to the unconscious by these theorists
(you can "prove" almost anything in this way)[3] as well as to cast
doubt on the privileging of early childhood development. Is the
mother/child relationship, important as it is, really the key to
later sexual promiscuity, depression, and self-absorbed jealousy?
Some think not. Indeed, for many feminists, at least, the Oedipus
and Electra complexes which underscore the importance of early
experience, are now, for the most part, deemed myths, creations
of an imaginative psychoanalytic literature that fail to illuminate
their own experience. This observation is not made to deny the
continuing value of psychoanalytic theory; it is offered only to
suggest a more critical appropriation of any such theory in the
future.

American Liberalism

Yet another way of diagnosing the human predicament takes its
cues from the radicalism of the 1960s and is a way favored by
many American liberals. Its chief sin is not the possession of
private property — although many liberals are genuinely appreciative of Marxist thought — nor the disruption of personality which
originates in childhood, but the absence of "politically correct
thinking" concerning race, sex, religion, color, creed, disability,
sexual orientation, national ancestry, or age. To be sure, it is one

thing to seek to improve society by eliminating racism, sexism, anti-Semitism, and other forms of bigotry. It is quite another thing, however, to mandate, in a dogmatic fashion, the specific policies, instruments, and social programs which supposedly will lead to the betterment of society. Two people, for example, may be equally concerned about eliminating racism in America, but they may differ as to what course of action will best achieve this end. But failure to fall into line not only with the favored social and political programs of the American left, but also with its "progressive" thinking is to commit a cardinal sin, and it often results in being labeled morally lacking.

Interestingly, though political correctness embraces a number of social groups and causes, each group within the broader movement often defines the essence of evil in terms of its own limited social perspective. For example, James Cone, an African-American theologian, responding to centuries of racial prejudice, maintains that the black/white distinction is nearly equivalent to the distinction good/evil. "Black theology," he writes, "will accept only a love of God which participates in the destruction of the white enemy."[4] And he adds clarifying his point: "The goal of Black Theology is the destruction of everything *white* so that black people can be alienated from alien gods."[5] Similarly, Albert Cleage in his work *Black Christian Nationalism* states: "The white man is a beast . . . [and] white Christianity is a bastard religion without a Messiah and without a God."[6]

It was not long before members of the black community themselves responded to such strident rhetoric, and several writers called for an approach which would eliminate racist thinking, whether white or black, and which would enhance the prospects for the integration of *all* peoples. Deotis Roberts, who is typical of this tendency, exclaims: "While Cone confesses an indifference to whites, *I care*. . . . It is my desire to speak to blacks and whites *separately,* but in the long run it is hoped that real intercommunication between blacks and whites may result."[7] Julius Lester, a black poet, astutely realized that if the black/white distinction epitomizes good and evil, then blacks will fail to recognize clearly their own shortcomings, for evil, by definition, is always a characteristic of the other. Lester observes: "Black theology is shameful because its spokesmen want us to believe that blacks are without sin."[8]

In some respects, feminist theology is similar in approach to black theology except that the female/male distinction now replaces the black/white one as the most useful window on human evil. Mary Daly, a former Roman Catholic who currently teaches theology at Boston College, has criticized many liberation movements precisely because, in her estimation at least, they have not been radical enough. In other words, these movements have failed to realize that patriarchy, a social system in which the father is the supreme authority, lies at the very heart of *all* human oppression. In her book *Beyond God the Father,* for example, Daly elaborates:

> [There are] movements which have liberation as their stated goal but which fix all their attention upon some deformity *within* patriarchy — for example, racism, war, poverty — rather than patriarchy itself, without recognizing sexism as root and paradigm of the various forms of oppression they seek to eradicate.[9]

Not surprisingly, Daly sees "sexual caste" as *the* "original sin" upon which "other manifestations of oppression are modeled."[10] However, the kind of criticism which Julius Lester leveled against radical black theologians can be translated and then applied with equal force to Daly's thought. That is, if the *essence* of evil is deemed to be patriarchy, then feminists will undoubtedly fail to appreciate their own evil, their own lust for power, and their own capacity for self-absorption, since by definition evil is considered to lie outside this preferred social circle. Indeed, Rosemary Ruether, a more moderate feminist theologian who is aware of these dangers, cautions:

> To the extent that they (oppressed groups) are not at all concerned about maintaining an authentic prophetic address to the oppressors; to the extent that they repudiate them as persons . . . they both abort their possibilities as a liberating force for the oppressors, and, ultimately, derail their own power to liberate themselves.[11]

THE PROBLEM ACCORDING TO THE BIBLE

So many modern lectures, graduation addresses, and articles on the op-ed page of leading newspapers still treat the issue of poverty and social justice in terms of the promise of socialism. So many volumes in the psychology section of neighborhood bookstores still presuppose the autonomous self and offer some version of the insight model, often packaged in the form of self-help, as the antidote to human malaise. And so many priests and preachers continue to argue from the pulpit on Sunday mornings that "enlightened views" (which means ones which essentially agree with their own) on race, gender, and class *constitute* the Gospel. Our modern age, in other words, discusses the traumas of the human condition in some quite predictable ways. Appeals to social science, or to ideology, or even to popular political and religious views are often the main ingredients of which contemporary assessments are made. Here the specialist is royalty and the intellectual rules. Here the very latest thought, the most up-to-date and relevant views are coveted. But can a different approach be taken, and one which will, perhaps, focus on a different and more penetrating level of analysis? Can an earlier culture, thousands of years old, have something important or relevant to say about the human condition? Can an ancient Hebrew community, who believed that their God Yahweh was Lord of history, instruct us twentieth-century Americans who are so technologically, if not culturally, sophisticated? Can the simple narratives of the Gospels reveal to us the nature of our condition? Simply put, can the stories of the Bible address the crucial issues concerning good and evil that people will face in the 1990s and beyond? Let's see.

The Old Testament Context

Generally speaking, evil may be defined as the destruction of what human beings value, whether that value be life, health, bodily integrity, reputation, or knowledge. For example, in the three options which we have considered so far, evil was portrayed as a very human problem: it involved either an oppressor dominating a victim, disharmony within the human psyche, or the

THE ROOT OF THE PROBLEM **21**

bourgeoisie aggressively exploiting the lower classes of society. In each instance, however, with the notable exceptions of black and feminist theology, little appeal was made to anything that transcends the human self or a society of selves.

The term "sin," on the other hand, though it is often equated with the term "evil," can be distinguished from it in one important respect. That is, evil can be understood exclusively as a human problem without any reference to God, as atheists and agnostics will testify, but sin can never be so understood. In a theological context, in the context presupposed by the term sin, human beings and their values are now not the only ingredients in the moral environment. God, a Being who can be distinguished from the human community, and who indeed transcends that community, is present as well, and the term "sin" takes account of that presence. Again, sin is evil not simply in the sight of human beings but, more importantly, it is evil *in the sight of God;* it is a "missing of the mark," a falling short of the *divine* intention.

Now when many people think of the biblical account of evil, they often have in mind a little story found in Genesis 3. To be sure, the story of Adam, Eve, and the serpent is a familiar one, even if its details are somewhat misunderstood or confused in popular culture (Eve, for example, did *not* eat an apple). However, many of those who have read this text carefully, have come away from the experience with a renewed appreciation for the beauty and wisdom of the Bible. For in remarkably simple language, in a gracious and easy style, the Holy Scriptures communicate rich and enduring truths. Put another way, the Bible offers not a lecture on evil, not a discourse on philosophy or metaphysics, not scientific or technical jargon, but a simple yet profound story which remarkably illuminates the human experience. As we begin to explore the Genesis account, we must pay attention to the dynamics of temptation and notice how well they ring true.

Take Genesis 3:1, for instance. Here the serpent, a principal character in the account, asks the woman: "Did God really say, 'You must not eat from any tree in the garden'?" The question is intriguing because it sows a seed of doubt in Eve's mind, a seed which will later blossom. But for now, and this is important, observe that the woman affirms that God said, "You must not eat fruit from the tree that is in the middle of the garden, and you must not touch it, or you will die" (3:2-3). However, if we take the prohibition of Genesis 2:16-17 as our guide ("You are free to eat from any tree in the garden; but you must not eat from the tree of the knowledge of good and evil, for when you eat of it you will surely die"), then Eve's response to the serpent can be judged nearly accurate, indicating that she really did know what was the will of God.

Losing the first battle, so to speak, the serpent tries another tactic: "You will not surely die. . . . For God knows that when you eat of it your eyes will be opened, and you will be like God, knowing good and evil" (Gen. 3:4-5). Actually, the serpent is much more cunning than initially supposed, for it does not simply tell the woman a boldfaced, outright lie, but intermixes a little truth and a little falsehood. On the one hand, it is true that if Adam and Eve eat of the forbidden tree, their eyes will be opened and they will be like God (in a certain sense), knowing good and evil. But, on the other hand, it is not true that they will not die; they surely will. Observe, also, that the serpent continues its cunning ways and builds on the seeds of doubt sown earlier by suggesting to Eve that perhaps God doesn't have her best interests in mind after all and, therefore, intentionally holds something back from her which is very valuable: she and her husband could be like God!

The next verse not only displays the subtle and enticing dynamics of temptation, but it also details humanity's descent into sin. However, the Fall occurs in a different place in the story than where, once again, popular mythology suggests. Observe the language in the following text: "When the woman saw that the fruit of the tree was good for food and pleasing to the eye, and also desirable for gaining wisdom, she took some and ate it. She also gave some to her husband, who was with her, and he ate it" (Gen. 3:6).

Is the sin of Eve and Adam that they have actually eaten from the tree of knowledge of good and evil, or have they sinned prior to this act? Is their disobedience, in other words, their willful self-assertion, the essence of sin or is it simply the manifestation, the public revealing of a prior act? In a real sense, has not the sin of Adam and Eve occurred much earlier in doubting the goodness of God, in failing to trust the Most High, and in descending to unbelief? Indeed, neither Adam nor Eve could have willfully disobeyed and rebelled, except that they had *already* separated themselves from God by their own lack of trust, by their own unbelief. Simply put, somewhere between the seduction of temptation and the eating of the fruit, Eve sinned in her heart. From that moment with its breach of trust, God, for Eve, was no longer God, no longer her Lord and Sovereign. Effects, therefore, must not be mistaken for causes.

THE NEW TESTAMENT CONTEXT

Though Genesis 3 is a good window on human evil, it would be a mistake for the Christian community to limit its discussion to this text; the New Testament must be explored as well. Emil Brunner, a twentieth-century Swiss theologian, affirmed that the church does not fully appreciate the hideousness of sin and evil until it considers, by way of contrast, the excellency of God's grace in Jesus Christ. In Romans 5, for instance, the Apostle Paul sets up a comparison between Adam and Christ. Note the differences in the following chart.

Adam	Christ
Many died by the trespass of one man (v. 15).	God's gift came by the grace of the one man, Jesus Christ, to overflow to the many (v. 15).
The result of one man's sin: judgment and condemnation (vv. 16, 18).	The gift followed many trespasses and brought justification (vv. 16, 18).
By the trespass of the one man death reigned (v. 17).	Those who receive God's gift will reign in life through the one man, Jesus Christ (v. 17).

Through the disobedience of one man, many were made sinners (v. 19).	Through the obedience of the one man, many will be made righteous (v. 19).
Sin reigned in death (v. 21).	Grace reigns through righteousness through Jesus Christ (v. 21).

This contrast, then, suggests that we need to proceed both positively and negatively. Negatively, Adam and Eve depict humanity gone awry, fallen into alienation and unbelief. God is no longer God for them; they have chosen the path of independence. Positively, Jesus Christ demonstrates what a restored humanity will look like in faith and holiness. Thus, ever in a proper relationship with the Father, the God/Man Jesus Christ submitted His will to the One in whom He *trusted:* "My Father, if it is possible, may this cup be taken from me. Yet not as I will, but as you will" (Matt. 26:39). In fact, there is no one throughout the pages of the Bible, Old Testament or New Testament, who said more about faith and trust (the opposite of unbelief) or who demonstrated its attractiveness better than Jesus Christ. Two passages give the reader a sense of just how Jesus ministered to people and what He saw as their most important need.

> On the last and greatest day of the Feast, Jesus stood and said in a loud voice, "If anyone is thirsty, let him come to me and drink. Whoever believes in me, as the Scripture has said, streams of living water will flow from within him" (John 7:37-38).

> Jesus said to her [Martha], "I am the resurrection and the life. He who believes in me will live, even though he dies; and whoever lives and believes in me will never die. Do you believe this?" (John 11:25-26)

This, then, is to view the problem positively, to display what humanity, through the bountiful grace of God in Jesus Christ, may become. Adam was alienated from God, isolated in fear, and trapped in unbelief; Jesus Christ, on the other hand, was free in

His trust of the Father. If the cure is faith, the disease must be unbelief.

THE CHURCH REFLECTS ON SIN

It is not possible, nor is it appropriate, to consider every different view on the nature of sin and evil which has surfaced in the church. However, what can be offered, given our space limitations, is a brief discussion of the major views which continue to be discussed today, as well as those which amplify and illustrate the theme of this chapter.

We begin with St. Augustine, a fifth-century Latin church father, whose views on the nature and transmission of sin had a significant impact on subsequent theology. For this bishop of Hippo, the essence of sin was concupiscence, a word which was used to translate the biblical term for lust or desire *(epithumia)* as in 1 Thessalonians 4:3-5: "It is God's will that you should be sanctified . . . that each of you should learn to control his own body in a way that is holy and honorable, not in passionate *lust* like the heathen who do not know God." Concupiscence, then, is an excessive longing, a craving for what is not ultimate, a desire for what is less than God. It can be understood either in terms of perverted self-love (pride) which is driven by inordinate desire or in terms of the rebellion which gives rise to such a perverted love.

Though Augustine conceived the nature of sin in terms of concupiscence and pride and therefore cannot be cited in support of the larger theme in this chapter, which sees sin essentially in terms of alienation and unbelief, his views must nevertheless be considered in any treatment of this topic because of his subtle, and sometimes not so subtle, association of sin and human sexuality. For instance, Swiss neo-orthodox theologian Emil Brunner writes:

> His [Augustine's] doctrine of Original Sin was directly connected with his doctrine of sexual concupiscence as the "primal" sin and of sexual procreation as the source of sin in every human being, above all in that of the new-born child.[12]

In one respect, what Brunner argues here is accurate, but in another respect it is not. Contrary to popular belief, Augustine did not specify sexual concupiscence or desire as *the* essence of sin; instead, he simply left it open and wrote along the lines of the general term concupiscence which can take many different forms of desire, sexual included. However, Brunner is correct when he notes that Augustine did, in fact, link the transmission of original sin from one generation to the other to human sexuality. Unfortunately, once this identification was made, it was not long before others began to identify human sexuality and sin to the point where the terms became virtually synonymous. And the famous proof text for this view was none other than Psalm 51:5: "Surely I was sinful at birth, sinful from the time my mother conceived me." Naturally, the spirituality which arises from this kind of judgment views the body and temporal existence in a largely negative manner and as the principal obstacles which must be overcome in order for the highest spirituality to occur. Although the strong association of sin and sexuality is a major theme in the life of the church, other views, especially those held by Irenaeus, for example, seem better able to account for both the goodness of creation — the Word became flesh — as well as the hideousness of sin.

Augustinian theology and the Neoplatonism which informed it held sway in the church throughout the Dark Ages. During the thirteenth century, however, the work of Aristotle was reappropriated in the West, and in the area of theology in particular, by Thomas Aquinas. On the question of evil, Thomas maintained that original sin is a disordered disposition which resulted from "the dissolution of the harmony which was once the essence of original justice."[13] But just what does this medieval language mean? In order to help his thirteenth-century readers (and perhaps us as well), Thomas draws an analogy between bodily sickness as a consequence of the loss of equilibrium and the disordered disposition (sin) which is the result of the loss of original justice. In other words, lack of original justice, the disruption of a harmonious relationship, robbed humanity of the subjection of its mind to God and this in turn gave rise to a disordered disposition and corrupt habits. The saintly scholar writes: "The whole order of original justice consisted in the subjection of man's will to God. . . . Disorder in any other part of his soul is therefore the consequence of his will turning away from God."[14] The fracture of the relationship between God and humanity, the rupture of trust that resulted in turning the will away from God, define the essence of sin in this view.

Although Thomas Aquinas is revered by the entire Christian community, he is celebrated in a special way by Roman Catholicism. In fact, Leo XIII, a nineteenth-century pope, directed Catholics to the study of this great thirteenth-century theologian in a special way. What is perhaps more interesting, however, is that Aquinas' views on original sin are not very different from those of some leading Protestant thinkers. John Calvin, for example, a Protestant Reformer from the sixteenth century, rejected the notion, contrary to popular belief, that pride was the root of evil and focused instead on the whole question of faithlessness. Examining the text of Genesis 3, Calvin explains: "Since the woman through unfaithfulness was led away from God's Word by the serpent's deceit, it is already clear that disobedience was the beginning of the Fall."[15] And again, "Adam would never have dared oppose God's authority unless he had disbelieved in God's Word."[16] Yet even more emphatically, the Genevan Reformer writes in his *Institutes of the Christian Religion:*

> Unfaithfulness, then, was the root of the Fall. But thereafter ambition and pride, together with ungratefulness, arose, because Adam by seeking more than was granted him shamefully spurned God's great bounty.[17]

Likewise, Martin Luther in his *Lectures on Genesis* which were written when the Reformation was already well underway concludes that Eve was urged on by the serpent to commit the sin of all sins, the one from which all else arises: namely, to doubt the Word and thereby forfeit trust in God. "Unbelief is the source of all sins;" Luther writes, "when Satan brought about this unbelief by driving out or corrupting the Word, the rest was easy for him."[18] Eve was led away from trust in the Word of God to idolatry. Moreover, Luther underscores this theme once again in his observation on Genesis 3 that "all evils result from unbelief or doubt of the Word and of God. For what can be worse than to disobey God and to obey Satan."[19]

A third major Protestant tradition, beyond the Reformed and Lutheran movements, also views the origin and essence of human evil in a comparable way. Like his predecessors, John Wesley, the father of Methodism, took great care to come to his own understanding of these matters in light of the biblical accounts. Beginning with Genesis 3, Wesley describes the fall of Eve in his sermon "The End of Christ's Coming," and maintains that Satan, as an external foil, mingled truth with falsehood so that "unbelief begot pride . . . it begot self-will."[20] Elsewhere, in his sermon "On the Fall of Man," the one-time Oxford fellow again underscores unbelief as the primal factor and exclaims, "Here sin began, namely, unbelief. 'The woman was deceived,' says the Apostle. She believed a lie: she gave more credit to the word of the devil than to the word of God."[21] For Wesley, then, as for his fellow Protestant leaders, the nature of human sin, its irreducible essence, is not pride, but, once again, unbelief. A lack of faith in God is the true foundation for the *subsequent* evils of pride and self-will. In other words, out of alienation and unbelief pride and self-will inevitably flow. That this assessment is correct is also borne out in Wesley's further comments as he considers the solution to the problem of human wickedness: "As Satan began his work in Eve by tainting her with unbelief, so the Son of God begins his work in man by enabling us to believe in him."[22]

Lastly, we turn to the work of Emil Brunner, which also highlights the essence of sin and human evil as unbelief and distrust of a Holy God. In his book, *The Christian Doctrine of Creation and Redemption,* Brunner explores the story of the Fall and points out that "evil, understood as sin, is a change in man's relation to God: it is the break in communion with God, due to distrust and defiance."[23] Interestingly, Brunner's major contribution to this broader discussion is that the essence or nature of sin is not a thing or substance at all, but a *relation.* Simply put, sin is a perverted relation to God; it is the attempt to be independent of God; it is humanity going its own way. It is the misguided endeavor, in its most subtle forms, to bring about redemption and healing apart from the Most High.

Such views on sin, no doubt, grew out of Brunner's understanding of the truth of the Bible which is preeminently concerned not with speculative or abstract truth, *I-It* truth (the truth of science), but with *I-Thou* truth, the truth of personal relations, what Brunner calls Divine/Human correspondence. To illustrate this last point, Brunner stresses that once creation occurs the God of the Bible is always the God of humanity. God, in other words, is never considered by Himself, abstractly, apart from humanity; nor is humanity ever considered by itself, but always in terms of its relation to a Holy God. Indeed, in one sense, humanity cannot help but be in relation to God. It is either in a proper relation to God in trust, submission, and obedience or else it is in an improper relation to God through alienation, rebellion, and sin. However, that sin is primarily a perverted *relation* characterized by distrust and a thirst for independence is Brunner's chief contribution to the larger discussion.

SOME OBSERVATIONS

Though we have defined the root of evil in terms of unbelief, this is not to suggest that the insights of Marx, Freud, and American liberal thought lack merit. Within the proper limits, and critically applied, all of these approaches represent useful and informative diagnostic tools. Indeed, part of the task of constructive theology in the future will be to demonstrate how some of the insights of Marxism, the fruits of a critically examined social scientific perspective, as well as social justice issues which pertain to race, sex, and economic status can be expressed through the biblical worldview, and in a way which will not undermine that perspective. Here the call will be for a synthesis of complementary approaches, one which will take into account the different levels of analysis of each approach, while recognizing that the deepest, most sophisticated rendering, one which literally gets to the heart of the problem, belongs to Scripture.

Similarly, the choice of unbelief as a prism through which to view the reality of evil does not mean that the Bible cannot be interpreted differently nor is it to deny that other views have surfaced in the church throughout its long and rich history. Our aim is to be informative, not dogmatic. Indeed, many theologians, past and present, have, like Augustine, deemed pride in the form of self-love as the very heart of evil. Nevertheless, while appreciating many of the insights which emerge from this perspective, we must reject it for three major reasons: First, it is not radical enough; it does not go to the very root of the problem. As the next chapter will demonstrate, pride is not the cause of unbelief, but its effect. Moreover, all the insights that emerge from considering pride as the root of evil can easily be gathered up by the view that evil is essentially unbelief, but the reverse is not true.

Second, as was noted briefly earlier, the Bible's prescription of repentance and faith for human evil suggests something about the nature of the disease. Belief, trust, and faith, therefore, are not only the antidotes for pride, greed, envy, lust, and a host of other sins, but these terms also address the far more fundamental issue of unbelief quite directly.

Third, viewing sin principally in terms of pride tends to foster and perpetuate the illusion that the viciousness of pride can be overcome by an increase in virtue, that the self, by becoming more moral and virtuous, can heal itself. But is pride, in the sense of making the self *the highest value* in life, a spiritual and theological problem indicative of a perverted relation to God, or is it simply a moral problem, a vice, something which can be addressed by men and women apart from God? It is this question, among others, which will be explored more thoroughly in the following chapter.

SUMMING UP

In this chapter we have entertained various models for reckoning with human evil. After pointing out the differing levels of analysis offered by each, we then reviewed the judgments offered by the Bible and concluded that it is actually more "radical" than other approaches in that it goes to the root of the problem, that is, how humanity is related to God. Indeed, we have argued that the unbelief and alienation which characterize an autonomous humanity, a humanity bent upon self-rule, is the source for all sorts of evil.

Accordingly, in the following chapter, we will begin to delineate the self-curvature, the sinful pride, which is an inevitable consequence of human independence from a God who is beyond us in both being and glory.

INDIVIDUAL OR GROUP REFLECTION QUESTIONS

1 Some have argued that ever since Karl Marx referred to religion as "the opium of the people," Christianity has been more especially intent on demonstrating its relevance to the world. Has such an intent led to a transformation of Christianity's message and its understanding of spirituality? If so, how so? If not, why not?

2 If poverty, racism, and sexism were somehow eliminated from the earth such that each person had enough of the necessities of life and each was respected as a person, would there then be any need for the church to preach: "Repent, the kingdom of God is at hand"?

3 Why is unbelief a root sin? Demonstrate how quite diverse evils can arise from this single source. Can men and women become free of this evil through their own efforts?

4 Explore thoroughly the ramifications of the following statement: "All sin is first and foremost sin against God." What will such a view add to each of the analyses considered in this chapter?

TWO

THE CONSTRUCTION OF THE KINGDOM OF SELF

The acts of the sinful nature are obvious . . . idolatry and . . . selfish ambition" (Gal. 5:19-20).

PRIDE: THE CONSEQUENCE OF UNBELIEF

If men and women are in a state of alienation from God, if they neither trust the Most High nor submit to His care, then they are truly alone. Lacking belief in God as the central value of their lives, people immediately set up "the kingdom of self"[1] in some form or other as a defense mechanism, growing ever dependent on their own resources. Put another way, once God is dethroned, self-will inevitably becomes king. Thus, the individual ego with its interests, drives, and intellect becomes the supreme value of life. It has become, as the serpent had promised, like God.

Unfortunately, this shift of allegiance from God to self seems so "natural" to some, and many elements in our culture actually reinforce it, sometimes in some very subtle ways. Take North American television, for instance. Although many critics complain of its excessive violence, its increasingly foul language, and its titillation of the senses, perhaps the most serious problem with this medium is its graphic presentation, day in and day out, of life without God. In the typical TV drama or sitcom, for example, God plays little if any role in the lives of the main characters. The leading men and women of the most popular television series neither pray to God nor do they talk much about going to church or synagogue. And in those rare instances when religion is treated, it is often either the butt of a joke or else its faults are greatly exaggerated (e.g., clergy are portrayed as buffoons, sexual deviants, or con artists).

Or take the well-worn American myth of rugged individualism which suggests that men and women, through their own craft and effort, can overcome any obstacle put in their way. Remarkably, this myth, in conjunction with others (e.g., Yankee ingenuity), predisposes us toward certain types of value judgments—judgments which, surprisingly enough, may move us away from the development of vital *communities* and from a serious faith in God. More to the point, Robert Bellah and others have argued recently in their book *Habits of the Heart* that the central problem of American life is rampant individualism. "It seems to us," Bellah observes, "that it is individualism, and not equality, as Tocqueville thought, that has marched inexorably through our history."[2]

Moreover, American individualism which can easily descend into self-centeredness is supported and held in place by an entirely new kind of literature that hardly existed twenty years ago. In most bookstores today, right next to the psychology section you will find an increasingly popular self-help section which some have affectionately called "the self-absorption section." To illustrate, Robert Ringer's book *Looking Out for #1*[3] (and you know who #1 is) which originally appeared in 1977 was not only on the *New York Times* bestseller list for an entire year, but it is still in print today. Other titles in this new genre include: Ringer's earlier book *Winning through Intimidation,*[4] *The Self-Talk Solution*[5] by Shad Helmstetter, and *Honoring the Self: The Psychology of Confidence and Respect*[6] by Nathaniel Branden. Interestingly, this last book has chapters on "Evolving toward Autonomy," and "Rational Selfishness" which express best, perhaps, the major theme of this new kind of literature.

Cultural forces like television, literature, and popular psychology can have a slow but damaging effect on the mind. The reigning values of our society expressed in these forces can almost imperceptibly craft our minds, consciences, and most basic orientations toward life. To be sure, it takes great intellectual effort to be even modestly aware of their imprint. To illustrate this, observe the following pairs of words and ask yourself which terms are positive and which are not.

autonomous ⟶	submissive
independent ⟶	dependent
proud ⟶	humble
free ⟶	obedient
self-reliant ⟶	relying on others (trust)
master ⟶	servant

If you are like most people, you probably prefer the words of the left-hand column to those of the right. The good news is that you are in the majority. The bad news, of course, is that the spirituality of the Bible emphasizes the right-hand column. Please note, however, that we are not implying that words like "independent," "proud," and "free" are necessarily negative, for they clearly are not. Within the proper limits, they too have significant value. They cause harm, however, when they orient us toward ourselves as the highest value in life, *prejudice* us against submission to and trust in God, and suggest that surrender, dependence, and humility are *always or are most often* negative.

In the discussion which follows, it is recognized that the term *pride* has many meanings, not all of which are bad. Consequently, pride in the sense of "satisfaction which grows out of accomplishment" is not the issue here. However, pride in the sense of excessive self-love is very much the issue and it constitutes one of the more significant obstacles to enjoying the rich grace of God.

THE BIBLICAL PERSPECTIVE

Though the Bible is the most popular book in history, it is a book which is seldom properly understood. Indeed, there are many different kinds of attitudes we can bring to the Bible, some of which will actually prevent us from seeing the grace and beauty of this literature. Some people, for instance, view the Bible as a burden, a yoke, or a book of "do's" and "don'ts" that is intent on limiting our freedom above all else. Others view the Scriptures as a deposit of wisdom, a treasure of insight, which if sought, will lead to lasting and deep happiness. Simply put, one person's burden is another person's gift. Attitude or approach is everything.

Continuing this line of thought, the authors of the Book of Proverbs believed that they were passing along to their readers not burdensome regulations or restrictive laws, but vital truths, which if appropriated, would save people from the suffering and struggle of learning life's most important lessons by trial and error. Indeed, it has often been said that fools are those who never learn from their experience. A wise person, however, is not only one who learns from experience, but one who, more importantly, learns from *instruction* as well.

Just what do the authors of the wisdom sayings of Proverbs teach? For one thing they caution against selfish pride and arrogance as ways which, for all their allure and attractiveness, will inevitably lead us away from God. Consider the counsel given in the following precepts.

"He mocks proud mockers, but gives grace to the humble."
(Prov. 3:34)

"I hate pride and arrogance, evil behavior and perverse speech."
(Prov. 8:13)

"When pride comes, then comes disgrace, but with humility comes wisdom." (Prov. 11:2)

"The Lord detests all the proud of heart. Be sure of this: They will not go unpunished. (Prov. 16:5)

"Pride goes before destruction, a haughty spirit before a fall."
(Prov. 16:18-19)

"Haughty eyes and a proud heart, the lamp of the wicked, are sin!" (Prov. 21:4)

In a similar fashion, the psalmist warns that the path of pride does not lead the self to wholeness and vitality, as is often supposed, but to darkness and godlessness. "In his pride the wicked does not seek him; in all his thoughts there is no room for God" (Ps. 10:4). Self-will and arrogance, then, storm the soul and displace its true center. They dethrone God in order to set up a petty monarch. Not surprisingly, it has been suggested that the word "ego" itself is actually an acronym for the phrase Easing God Out. The psalmist would have understood such wisdom.

Now one of the truly perplexing things about human evil (and pride as a manifestation of evil) is its tendency to appear as other than it is. Evil seeks to remain hidden, mysterious, and elusive. It often involves an act of deception, a lie on many levels, both to the self and to others. Again, evil often masquerades as the good; it pretends that it is well-motivated, that it is gracious, kind, and loving, but its fruits do not lie. To illustrate, in the New Testament there is perhaps no greater example of human evil masking itself than in the lives of the Pharisees. In the Gospel of Matthew, for instance, Jesus calls these religious leaders "blind guides," "blind fools," "snakes," "brood of vipers," but most often He simply refers to them as hypocrites. The average reader, however, probably misses or mistakes the evil which Jesus addressed in His rebuke. The Pharisees were indeed hypocrites, play actors, but not in a way that we might initially expect. Their evil was much more hidden than that, and it took a Jesus to unmask it. It was not a matter of the Pharisees being virtuous in public and vicious in private. This is not really the dividing line of their hypocrisy; the fault lies elsewhere. In fact, if these same religious leaders were alive today, we would probably identify them as virtuous, as concerned, and as the pillars of the community. But remember Jesus called them evil in the sharpest terms possible. Why? The account of Matthew gives us some clues.

First of all, the Pharisees loved the place of honor at banquets, the most important seats in the synagogues, and to be greeted as "Rabbi." They loved to be, in other words, the center of attention. Second, Jesus stated that these religious leaders were full of greed and self-indulgence. In most instances, they sought to profit themselves, to bask in the attention and approval of others, and to suffer no competition as they managed the religious life of the Jews—which is why, by the way, they did not take kindly to either John the Baptist or Jesus. And third, the Pharisees appeared to people as righteous (that's why their evil was so hard to discern), but in their hearts they were full of hypocrisy and wickedness.

What these clues suggest, then, is that the Pharisees were nothing less than idolaters. No, they did not bow down to molten idols or to statues of goddesses, but they did substitute the love of self for the love of God. Put another way, they had violated the first and most important commandment of all, "I am the Lord your God. . . . You shall have no other gods before me" (Ex. 20:2-3). Hiding behind virtue and respectability, the Pharisees continually fed an enormous self-love that was boundless in its appetite and destructive in its effects. Consider this, here were the religious leaders of Israel at the helm, so to speak, and instead of guiding the ship to the shore of the God of Abraham, Isaac, and Jacob, they instead turned in at their own port! The whole religious apparatus of Judea was set up for themselves as revealed in their own remarks: "If we let him [Jesus] go on like this, everyone will believe in him, and then the Romans will come and take away both *our* place (the temple) and *our* nation" (John 11:48). Little wonder Jesus' rebuke was so harsh.

Though the New Testament repeatedly warns against the sin of pride as in Paul's counsel to the Romans: "Do not think of yourself more highly than you ought" (Rom. 12:3), this sin is so easy to fall into precisely because it appears to be not only an enhancement of the self, but it even appears, at times, to be downright admirable. The goodness of a God-given intellect, for instance, can be slowly perverted and altered from its course through self-absorbed delight in one's own learning and insights. Regrettably, this is a fault characteristic not only of some secular academics, but of theologians and clergy as well. Here the goodness of knowledge, and of the discipline necessary to attain it, have been diverted from their proper course of the glorification of God to a glorification of self. And though the contemporary church is blessed with many great intellectuals, truly a gift from God, how many theologians are known and valued not only for their intellect, but also for their sanctity, for having the mind which was in Christ Jesus? (cf. Phil. 2:5)

Lest there be misunderstanding, we are by no means advocating anti-intellectualism, for the church greatly needs her scholars. But, on the other hand, we do renounce intellectual pride in all its forms along with the claim, made by some modern scholars, that one has to be an expert on the higher criticism of the Bible as well as a great intellect in order to understand the Gospel of Jesus Christ. Recently, J. Edward Carothers maintained in his *Paralysis of Mainstream Protestant Leadership* that the average dedicated layperson today can no longer effectively teach a Sunday School class because he or she lacks sufficient training in the fields of both modern theology and biblical criticism.[7] However, if the end of a Sunday School class is to understand the latest abstract, theoretically demanding, speculative thought of the theologians, then perhaps Carothers is correct. But if the purpose of the class is to study the Scriptures so that all will encounter the knowledge of God's love in Jesus Christ, then dedicated laypeople will make some of the very best teachers. The Gospel message remains remarkably simple, and for that very reason, is profound. And precisely because it is so simple it often eludes the sophisticated. Recall the words of Jesus: "I praise you, Father, Lord of heaven and earth, because you have hidden these things from the wise and learned, and revealed them to little children. Yes, Father, for this was your good pleasure" (Matt. 11:25-26).

Anyone who has ever read the entire New Testament soon realizes that its judgments are not necessarily the same as those of modern culture, nor even of the contemporary church. In fact, there seems to be a kind of reversal of values which takes place in this literature. That is, what's good from the New Testament's perspective is often "bad" according to modern culture, and vice versa. Our own American society, for instance, teaches us in many ways that it is much better to receive than to give, to be served than to serve, and to promote oneself rather than to seek humility. Jesus, however, turns this distorted, hostile, and lonely world upside down. He taught His disciples that "unless you become as a little child, you will never enter the kingdom of heaven" (Matt. 18:3). He also counseled that "the greatest among you will be your servant" (Matt. 23:11-12). And to top it all, Jesus proclaimed, "But many who are first will be last, and the last first" (Mark 10:31).

Beyond this, the ethic of Jesus Christ conflicts with what is often called common sense, because in one view the self is at the center of things; but in the other it is not. Different beginnings, in other words, lead to different endings. From the perspective of the selfish ego, humility looks like a diminishment, a loss, a dying of the self (and in a sense it is). To the Christ-centered ego, however, humility is coveted not only for the peace which it brings, but also because it truly liberates. One is now free to serve the neighbor energetically, to wash the feet of others, to care for the neglected without immediately asking "what's in it for me?" In short, one is free to love; one is free to enjoy the greatest liberty of all.

Again, this reversal of values is at the heart of the difference between the kingdom of God and the kingdom of self, and it is graphically expressed in Jesus' triumphal entry into Jerusalem shortly before His crucifixion and death. To be sure, Jesus of Nazareth taught about the kingdom of God in many ways: through stories and parables, through His actions of healing the sick and raising the dead, and through His unswerving trust of the Father. But it is perhaps this image of a man riding a donkey which, because of its simplicity, is able to slip by our normal value system, only to reveal later on what the kingdom of God is all about. Imagine this: here is a road which descends to the Mount of Olives, and it is lined with people who are joyfully praising God and shouting:

"Blessed is the king who comes in the name of the Lord!" (Luke 19:38)

"Peace in heaven and glory in the highest!" (Luke 19:38)

So enthusiastic are these people that they desire to give even greater honor to this man and so they begin to cut down branches from the trees and spread them on the road, amidst cries of "Hosanna to the Son of David! Blessed is he who comes in the name of the Lord! Hosanna in the highest!'' (Matt. 21:9) Many of the sights and sounds of this spectacle suggest that a triumphant king is being honored—and so He is. But here is a king with a difference, for Jesus rides not some powerful dark stallion, the favorite of the Caesars and Roman generals, but a donkey. Suddenly, the image begins to take effect, a window on the kingdom of God opens ever so slightly. This king is quite unlike other kings. He is lowly and humble. Luke's account of the event indicates that the crowd praised Jesus "for all the miracles they had seen" (Luke 19:37). But would they have continued to praise Jesus if they had realized what riding a donkey symbolized? "Say to the Daughter of Zion, 'See, your king comes to you, gentle [humble] and riding on a donkey, on a colt, the foal of a donkey' " (Matt. 21:5). Perhaps not.

THE MODERN CHURCH

If contemporary preaching in some denominations is any indication of the health of the church, then we must conclude that the patient is ill but doesn't know it. Indeed, the average fare on Sunday mornings is often composed, first of all, of some form of the message that God loves you "just as you are." But this message, if not properly presented, can be downright dangerous. Tell self-absorbed people that God loves them and they will hardly thank you for your trouble. "Of course, God loves me!" comes the reply. Here the beauty of the Gospel that God does indeed love sinners runs the risk of being taken for granted and, consequently, of not being properly understood. Note that the problem here is not the message itself, which is glorious, but the timing. Some preachers say the right thing but at the wrong time. Preaching the love of God without also preaching the law of God *first* can have the miserable result of comforting people in their sins and leaving their own sense of righteousness hardly shaken. Preaching the love of God without also calling for fundamental reform of the human heart can reaffirm the soul's presumptuous self-indulgence, leaving the kingdom of self undisturbed.

Second, the proclamation of God's love on Sunday mornings is usually followed by a broad appeal for moral living. "Be a good person; be concerned; be an active member of the community; contribute generously to the church" are the phrases often trumpeted from the pulpit. This is all very good counsel, but there is a problem here; namely, that these appeals never move beyond the moral dimension; that is, they leave the I at the center of its world as the principal doer of the good—with predictable results. For some pastors, however, this is precisely as it should be since they virtually equate religion and morality in a way reminiscent of Kant and Ritschl. But religion can, after all, be distinguished from morality not only in the sense that not all morality is religious, but also, and more importantly, in the sense that religion may, at times, move beyond the realm of morality to include a genuinely spiritual dimension. To be sure, spirituality includes something higher than conventional morality, something loftier than mere religion. Remember the Pharisees were very moral people, and no one could possibly accuse them of not being religious! But, as Jesus warned, "unless your righteousness surpasses that of the Pharisees and the teachers of the law, you will certainly not enter the kingdom of heaven" (Matt. 5:20).

What, then, is spirituality and how is it to be distinguished from religion? Interestingly enough, according to some scholars, the term spirituality did not come into use until fairly recently. "Spirituality as a word is apparently French Catholic in origin," writes Charles Hambrick-Stowe, "perhaps going back only to the seventeenth century in that language."[8] In its current and popular usage, however, it describes, according to Gordon Wakefield, "those attitudes, beliefs, practices which animate or inform people's lives and help them to reach out towards super-sensible realities."[9] Matthew Fox, a Roman Catholic theologian and Dominican, contends that spirituality is about roots. "For all spirituality," he writes, "is about living a nonsuperficial and therefore a deep, rooted, or radical (from radix, root) life." Roots are collective and not merely personal—much less are they private or individualized.[10] And David Ray Griffin, for his part, no doubt influenced by Paul Tillich, maintains that the term spirituality refers "to the ultimate values and meanings in terms of which we live."[11] It is also customary, Griffin adds, "to use spirituality in a stricter sense for a way of life oriented around an ultimate mean-

ing and around values other than power, pleasure, and possession."[12]

Though the term spirituality, as we will employ it in this book,
resonates with each of the definitions noted above, there are two
aspects which we will take particular care to develop. First, spirituality always involves *transcendence* in a way that morality does
not; it reaches out, to use Wakefield's phrase, toward "super-
sensible realities"; it aims at someone or something higher than
the self. Put another way, spirituality graciously surpasses the
limits and powers of the all-too-human ego to partake of the rich
life of a transcendent God. As such, it involves living outside of
oneself, beyond oneself, to enjoy a larger circle of meaning. Luther said it well: "I live in God through faith and in my neighbor
through love." Spirituality also helps us to transcend our excessive group commitments, to go beyond ethnocentrism and other
forms of group glorification. As such, we begin to see a larger
perspective than we had previously imagined. Moreover, spirituality explores those questions, often neglected in the modern era,
which pertain to *all* human beings as they confront the awful
realities of their own finite and limited existence, such matters as
guilt, anxiety, meaning, purpose, and the most weighty matter of
all, death.

Second, spirituality is radical, as Matthew Fox has noted, since
it focuses on the root of the problem with human beings. It not
only calls the self into question in a way that conventional morality does not, but it also cuts through the less-than-ultimate un-
derstandings of evil which are rife both in the church and in the
broader culture by taking into account the deepest recesses of
the human heart. But how many times have we heard a truly
prophetic word from the pulpit on Sunday morning, a word which
goes beyond mere moralism or talking about *other* people's faults,
a favorite form of self-righteousness, but cries out in anguish like
the Prophet Isaiah, aware of the "distance" between God and
humanity: "Woe to me! . . . I am ruined! For I am a man of
unclean lips, and I live among a people of unclean lips"? (Isa. 6:5)
None are fit to be prophets, until they have reckoned with their
own evil; none are fit to ascend the pulpit until they have caught
a vision of themselves in the sight of a holy God. What an

awesome calling.

Lest there be misunderstanding, we do affirm that healthy, vibrant religion includes morality and should ever promote moral behavior. Our point, however, is that morality does not constitute the entirety of religion. In a real sense, the difference between religion which places a premium on spirituality and one which does not can be seen in their dissimilar treatments of the problem of pride, our present subject. To illustrate, *spiritual* religion sees pride as a perverted *relation;* the whole being is out of harmony with God through unbelief and rebellion. *Conventional* religion, on the other hand, sees little of this evil dynamic, but views pride simply as a vice, a character defect or fault which will respond to some moral reform project. Again, spiritual religion maintains that the sinful self is the problem, that evil informs the whole character. Conventional religion, on the contrary, contends that an *aspect* of the self is at fault, and it, therefore, continues to uphold, in the face of much contrary evidence ("The heart is deceitful above all things and beyond cure. Who can understand it?" Jer. 17:9), the essential goodness of the self. Beyond this, spiritual religion underscores that apart from sanctifying grace, the will is divided and that the self, consequently, lacks integration. Conventional religion, however, fails to see that the will is divided; it, therefore, assumes the essential integrity of the self except for its vices, and it accomplishes all this by compartmentalizing and thereby minimizing evil.

But perhaps the most important difference between these two approaches is that spiritual religion affirms that the self *cannot* solve the problem of the self, which in this instance is sinful pride, precisely because the self is the problem. Conventional religion, on the other hand, naively assumes that the self can rid itself of pride, or that it can at least make sufficient improvement in this area. It, consequently, mistakes the depth of evil with which it deals. The following chart summarizes the differences in approach:

Pride as a Spiritual Problem	*Pride as a Moral Problem*
(1) Pride is a relation.	Pride is a vice.

(2) The self is the problem.	An aspect of the self is the problem.
(3) Evil informs the whole character (though the person is not totally evil).	Evil is an aspect of character (the essential goodness of the self).
(4) Painfully experiences a divided will.	Fails to see that the will is divided.
(5) Evil is seen for what it is.	Evil is minimized.
(6) Lacks integration (integrity).	Assumes integrity except for its vices; compartmentalizes evil.
(7) The self cannot solve the problem of pride (because the self is the problem).	The illusion that the self can solve the problem of pride.

Sadly, instead of calling the kingdom of self into account, many fashionable pastors seem to have thought of new ways to enlarge the sense of self of their congregations by sensitizing them, by instructing them to take offense easily, by enabling them to feel pain at the slightest infringement of their rights, and by encouraging them to criticize sharply those who view matters differently, ever forgetting that they serve a *crucified* Lord. These up-to-date pastors have schooled their flocks to become more assertive not less, to demand their rights on any occasion and at most any cost, and to champion all sorts of doubtful social and political causes. Becoming a prophet has never taken so little time. Becoming a spiritual person has never been so easy.

It is not a matter of the modern church lacking the resources to address the real needs of its congregations as they struggle with the questions of meaning, guilt, anxiety, fear, self-destructiveness, and death. To be sure, the contemporary church rests on a rich spiritual tradition, which though often neglected, now needs to be earnestly reappropriated. As an aid to this larger task, we will explore the church's rich treasure of spiritual classics which have been drawn, in an ecumenical fashion, from a diversity of traditions. These various works are all united in their emphasis on the value of personal transformation as the prerequisite for the most vital and engaging spirituality. They offer a whole Gospel, a kerygma which touches all dimensions of life, which goes to the core of the problem, and which, therefore, does not discount piety and devotion to God in the name of relevance.

A RICH LEGACY:
THE SPIRITUALITY OF THE UNIVERSAL CHURCH

We begin naturally with the early church, a time when the cost of being a Christian was quite high. Not only did Nero persecute Christians and charge them with all sorts of lies, but the emperors Domitian, Decius, and Diocletian all saw fit to abuse those who professed faith in Jesus Christ. In time, however, the persecution of Christians in the Roman Empire began to wane as Constantine and later Theodosius the Great looked more favorably on the church. Thus, as godly men and women no longer suffered "the second baptism" of martyrdom as an expression of their rich commitment to Jesus Christ, the spiritually earnest began to experiment with new ways of devotion. Some Christians, for instance, reacting to the spiritual laxity which emerged as a result of the church's accommodation with the empire, retreated from society and lived either as hermits (anchorites) or in communities (cenobites). This new form of spiritual devotion, known broadly as Christian monasticism, developed in the primitive church under the guidance of Anthony (251–356) and Pachomius (287–346). Later on, in the sixth century, Benedict of Nursia began to bring more order to the movement, and he crafted a *monastic rule* which was used to govern the daily life of communal (cenobitic) monasteries.[13] Even today the spiritually serious, both Roman Catholic and Protestant, can greatly profit from the wisdom of this early spiritual father. As will be evident shortly, the spiritual emphases of Benedict are no less relevant now than they were in the sixth century.

At the heart of the Benedictine Rule, which was created to provide godly direction for monks, is the idea of lowliness. The central chapter of the Rule details twelve steps or stages of humility, the first one being obedience. To become little in one's own eyes, Benedict teaches, to consider others as better than oneself (cf. Phil. 2:3), to temper the self's unending and excessive demands for enlargement, is the way to real peace not only within oneself, but within a community as well.

In a similar fashion, centuries later, Bernard, a Cistercian abbot who established a monastic community at Clairvaux, realized that self-love in various forms — some more evident than others — stifles our love of God, a love without which it is *impossible* to love our neighbor as we ought. The love of God, then, devotion to the Supreme Being, is absolutely necessary for spiritual development and for realizing the kingdom of God in this world. In his work, *On Loving God,* for instance, Bernard lists four degrees of love.

(1) We love ourselves for our own sake.
(2) We love God for our own sake.
(3) We love God for His sake.
(4) We love ourselves for God's sake.[14]

Given these degrees of love, how much of our own love is colored by how well God will bless us either in this life or in the one to come? How much of our love of the Holy One of Israel is deflected by anxiety over mundane concerns or over what Maslow has called maintenance needs? How often has our resentment or complaints of injustice smothered our adoration of the Sovereign Lord? Who, in other words, loves God for what He is, not for what He can do for us? Again, who is so forgetful of self that he or she loves God for His own sake, without qualification, and unspoiled by any self-interest? And what could it possibly mean to love ourselves for God's sake? Can we even fathom Bernard's fourth level of love?

The theme of the love of God, so richly displayed in the work of Bernard, continued to be a major theme in the writings of medieval scholars and mystics. Accordingly, in the thirteenth century, Thomas Aquinas, the leading theologian of the age, reworked an argument from Augustine and maintained that sinners love temporal goods excessively, thus displacing God, because they love themselves excessively, the most common form of idolatry. In a similar fashion, in the next century, Jan Van Ruysbroeck affirmed in his work *The Sparkling Stone* that there are many who serve God not out of love, but out of fear.

But perhaps the most thorough critique of human evil during the Middle Ages was neither by the period's leading theologian nor by one of its greatest mystics, but by an anonymous writer, the author of the *Theologia Germanica.* To be sure, anyone who has ever taken the trouble to read this spiritual classic will quickly realize that the author seeks to communicate deep spiritual truths to as broad an audience as possible through the use of clear language and also through repetition. Accordingly, the phrase "I, Mine, Me, and Self and the like," recurs throughout in order to drive home the major thesis of the work as typified by the following excerpt.

> I answer that a man should so stand free, being quit of himself, that is, of his I, and Me, and Self, and Mine, and the like, that in all things, he should no more seek or regard himself, than if he did not exist, and should take as little account of himself as if he were not. . . .[15]

According to the *Germanica,* Adam, the old man, is dominated by the I, Me, Self, Mine, and the like, and therefore continually operates out of self-will. If this is the case with Adam, the antitype of Christ, then who is Jesus, and how is He the light of the world? The *Germanica* explains: "Yea, Christ's human nature was so utterly bereft of Self . . . and was [therefore] nothing else but 'a house and habitation of God.' "[16] In addition, this fourteenth-century work underscores that the light of Christ, His deep beauty and humility, is not as easily communicated as some might initially expect. Neither intellectual development nor holding certain views about justice necessarily translates into spiritual development. "Let no one," this German classic advises, "suppose that we may attain to this true light and perfect knowledge or life of Christ by much questioning, or by hearsay, or by reading and study. . . ."[17] Why? Because the wisdom of Christ is most bitter to the self-centered life. Consequently, personal spiritual transformation, always a result of the grace of God, is absolutely necessary in order for the deeper truths of Christ to be known. Simply put, one must *become* lowly (not just talk about it) in order to appreciate the highest; one must *become* poor in spirit in order to acquire true riches; one must *become* little in one's own eyes in order to see the glory of God. The *Germanica* elaborates: "when a man hath this poor and humble spirit, he cometh to see and understand aright."[18]

Interestingly enough, it was none other than Martin Luther, the engine of the Reformation, who revived and popularized this medieval classic. Concerning the *Theologia Germanica,* Luther wrote: "To boast with my old fool, no book except the Bible and St. Augustine has come to my attention from which I have learned more about God, Christ, man, and all things."[19] And the influence of this medieval work can be seen in Luther's own spiritual writings as he taught that self-curvature, a turning in on oneself as the highest value, is the inevitable result of sin and unbelief. In his *Heidelberg Disputation,* written in 1518, Luther cautions against the idolatry of playing God, of setting oneself up as an idol to be worshiped and adored: "Let God (not the self) be God," he thundered.[20]

Similarly, John Calvin maintained that blind self-love is innate in all people: "Nothing pleases man more than the sort of alluring talk that tickles the pride that itches in his very marrow."[21] In his *Institutes of the Christian Religion,* he observes:

> There is, indeed, nothing that man's nature seeks more eagerly than to be flattered. Accordingly, when his nature becomes aware that its gifts are highly esteemed, it tends to be unduly credulous about them. It is thus no wonder that the majority of men have erred so perniciously in this respect . . . they are most freely persuaded that nothing inheres in themselves that deserves to be considered hateful.[22]

Continuing this line of thought, during the Enlightenment of the eighteenth century, John Wesley, the leader of the Methodists, detailed the ingredients of what we have called the kingdom of self in his sermon "The Deceitfulness of the Human Heart." In this piece, Wesley cautions against either thinking of our-selves more highly than we ought to, a common problem, or glorying in something which we have received from the hands of God as though we had not received it from Him.[23] Add to this Wesley's counsel against independence and self-will, and seeking happiness outside of God, and the picture which begins to emerge reveals that this British evangelical took seriously the whole question of inward religion and personal reformation as the only suitable antidote to idolatry.

Though John Wesley took great pains to demonstrate the rea-sonableness of the religion he preached (the love of God and neighbor) in his treatise *An Appeal to Men of Reason and Religion,* he could hardly stem the tide, even in his own country, of the spirit of self-sufficiency which had emerged during the eighteenth century. And though the Age of Reason was a boon in many respects, its emphasis on human autonomy (independence) could easily render unattractive the notion of submission to a Holy God, a crucial element in spirituality. Bear in mind that this last aspect of self-sufficiency, and its ramifications, is likewise part of the legacy which the Enlightenment has bequeathed to its heirs, to the nineteenth and twentieth centuries.

Despite these broader trends, which at times have issued in self-proclaimed atheism (Feuerbach, Nietzsche, Marx, Freud), our own age has not been without its spiritual giants within Roman Catholicism and Protestantism as well. In the former tra-dition Thomas Merton, like Benedict of Nursia and Bernard of Clairveaux before him, highlighted the crucial value of humility in becoming a spiritual person. In his work, *New Seeds of Contempla-tion,* for instance, the Trappist monk writes:

> It is almost impossible to overestimate the value of true humility and its power in the spiritual life. For the beginning of humility is the beginning of blessedness and the consummation of humility is the perfection of all joy. Humility contains in itself the answer to all the great problems of the life of the soul.[24]

In addition, Merton's courage in the face of popular twentieth-century trends is demonstrated as he critiques the kind of spirituality that is preoccupied with the distribution of limited material goods. Undoubtedly, his assessment of this struggle and its ultimate consequence will come as a surprise to some. Merton exclaims:

> What is the "world" that Christ would not pray for, and of which He said that His disciples were in it but not of it? The world is the unquiet city of those who live for themselves and are therefore divided against one another in a struggle that cannot end, for it will go on eternally in hell. It is the city of those who are fighting for possession of limited things and for the monopoly of goods and pleasures that cannot be shared by all.[25]

The words of this Roman Catholic cleric should give us all pause. How many times have we championed a cause or pressed for "our rights" or cried "injustice" when behind such calls for action was not the love of God and neighbor, but a greedy, grasping, and envious desire for our own enhancement. Arguments for justice, in other words, pleas for fairness, can *at times* become the bricks and mortar with which to build the kingdom of self. Spirituality, then, not only calls for a penetrating assessment of our own motivations, but it also calls for rigorous honesty.

From a monastery in Bardstown, Kentucky we move to cosmopolitan New York City; from the silence of the Trappists we move to the bustle of the United Nations; and from the thoughts of a very private man we move to the spiritual reflection of a very public man. Indeed, rich spirituality can be found in so many different places — and sometimes where you least expect it. When he first arrived in New York in the early 1950s to assume his duties at the United Nations, Dag Hammarskjöld appeared to be just another agnostic humanist. It came as something of a surprise, then, when the manuscript *Markings,* which will no doubt become a spiritual classic, was discovered in his apartment shortly after his death. In this work, the Swedish native offers a penetrating analysis of spirituality and observes that self-centeredness is the great destructive force of human life. He reasoned that to lose one's self in God is to discover self as it was meant to be.

But what is truly noteworthy about Hammarskjöld's approach is that he could have easily followed many of his peers by discussing the questions of good and evil almost exclusively in terms of well-worked political categories: lower class/upper class, rich/poor, and so on. But Hammarskjöld refused. Instead his thought and analysis went much deeper than the sociological or political level to become truly radical: that is, he considered the anthropological question, the self-absorption of *all* men and women as providing, perhaps, the most important clue to the human predicament.

In light of the preceding, it is evident that many spiritual mentors, from the pages of the New Testament to the writings of Dag Hammarskjöld, have repeatedly cautioned humanity against choosing the path of independence and autonomy, knowing full well that such an attempt at liberation will inevitably lead to the greatest and cruelest of all bondages, the tyranny of self. However, as significant as the problems of excessive personal self-love are, group or social egoism is perhaps a more difficult and serious problem simply because groups have far more opportunity and power to execute their will. And there is, perhaps, no theologian in the twentieth century who has taken this problem of group evil, the compounding of selfishness, more seriously than Reinhold Niebuhr, the last spiritual tutor we shall consider.

In 1932, four years after Niebuhr was appointed Professor of Christian Ethics at Union Theological Seminary in New York, he published the ground-breaking book *Moral Man and Immoral Society* which was read not only by theologians, as expected, but also by historians, sociologists, and political scientists who all found its basic thesis intriguing. In this book, Niebuhr maintains, in his perceptive way, that a sharp distinction must be drawn between the moral and social behavior of individuals and of social groups in light of the "brutal character of the behavior of all human collectives, and the power of self-interest and collective egoism in all intergroup relations."[26] In other words, Niebuhr is suggesting that the shift from the individual to the group represents not an arithmetic increase in egoism, but a geometric increase. If individuals are selfish, groups are even more so. Niebuhr writes:

As individuals, men believe that they ought to love and serve each other and establish justice between each other. As racial, economic and national groups they take for themselves, whatever their power can command.[27]

Moreover, in many of his other works, like *The Children of Light and the Children of Darkness* (1944) and *Christian Realism and Political Problems* (1953), Niebuhr further substantiates his larger thesis by pointing out that groups almost unswervingly pursue their own limited ends even when confronted with the knowledge that their own goals are at the expense of the good of other groups or at the expense of the good of the whole. "When power is robbed of the shining armor of political, moral and philosophical theories by which it defends itself," the American theologian wryly notes, "it will fight on without armor."[28]

In light of Niebuhr's description of the ethical characteristics of groups, it comes as something of a surprise to learn that some leaders in the contemporary church, which should be aiming at the universal love of Christ, have instead chosen to empower specific interest groups at the expense of others. For whatever reason, they have refused to note the self-serving arguments of preferred groups and movements by exempting them from the kinds of moral and intellectual critiques that are often applied to others. However, blind loyalty to a partisan movement, regardless of the reason, is not only a violation of love, and thus divides the body of Christ, but it is also an apt description of prejudice. In short, it is simply irrational to contend that prejudice can be eliminated by practicing prejudice. Richard Paul, a leader in the Critical Thinking movement, explains.

Prejudice nearly always exists in obscured, rationalized, socially validated, functional forms. It enables people to sleep peacefully at night even while flagrantly abusing the rights of others. It enables people to get more of what they want, or get it more easily. It is often sanctioned with pomp and ceremony. It sometimes appears as the very will of God. It is not mere coincidence that most groups concerned with prejudice concern themselves with the prejudice of *others*.[29]

Lest this last observation be read as an instance of political conservativism, it must be pointed out that spirituality, in its attentiveness to the human condition, critiques selfishness *wherever it is found,* both in individuals and in groups, among conservatives and liberals alike, within the Republican party as in the Democratic party, among men as well as women, with the rich as with the poor, both within and outside the church. It knows of no preferential options; it has no favored interest groups; it is not dominated by ideology. On the contrary, it remains both critical and free. It is critical in the sense that it is not deceived as various groups cloak their own will to power behind rational and moral arguments, as they seek to gain a greater share of society's limited goods at the expense of others. It is free in the sense that it is committed to the universal love of God (the kingdom of God) as the only value which can transcend the tyranny of self and the tribalisms of group life. It affirms, in other words, a radical monotheism which spells judgment for all groups which seek to paint their own limited causes and interests as ultimate, which seek to make their own narrow perspectives a universal one. Niebuhr elaborates:

> Inevitably, the exaltation of the class [or any other grouping for that matter], as the community of most significant loyalty, is justified by the proletarian [or others] by attaching universal values to his class. He does not differ from the privileged classes in attempting this universalization of his particular values.[30]

Admittedly, this kind of deep and critical spirituality can have a "braking effect" on some very credible claims of injustice simply because it makes one (or the group) painfully aware of one's own self-interest and deceit. And this is precisely where spirituality looks most conservative. However, spirituality does not foster, as is mistakenly supposed, naïveté nor passivity. That is, it is neither deceived with respect to the aims of *other* selves and groups nor does it allow the destructive egoism of *other* individuals and oppressive movements to go unchecked. It will not, for example, sit by idly while the poor are fleeced by "the respectable." But neither will it romanticize the poor, viewing them as the locus of all that is good. Here the larger good of the kingdom of God, universal love, will constrain it to speak out in a truly inclusive, seasoned, and balanced prophetic voice—a voice which is not, for the most part, self-righteous, but which has been tempered by a realization of its own evil. For this reason a rich and sensitive spirituality which is oriented toward God through transcendence and toward humanity through awareness of the dynamics of the human heart, can be remarkably relevant in a hurting world. It can move us beyond the limitations of self and groups in order that we may truly love God and our neighbor, the greatest liberty of all.

SUMMING UP

In this chapter we have briefly explored how culture can almost imperceptibly move us down a road toward sinful pride and forgetfulness of God. By way of contrast, we have considered how the Bible and church tradition challenge the self-orienting values celebrated in contemporary society. And finally, we entertained a few definitions of spirituality which emphasize transcendence; that is, definitions which highlight a movement *from* self and our preferred social group *to* God and neighbor. Indeed, becoming spiritual, living the Christian life in its depth, will be remarkably liberating (as we will see in subsequent chapters), but it will also involve great risk, for it will ultimately challenge our world at its very foundations by calling for nothing less than a new center. The monarch of the kingdom of self, in other words, must abdicate.

Nevertheless, that abdication—as you might have guessed—will not come easily. Indeed, in the next chapter we will explore how the self attempts to hide from its true condition, its central problem, by "losing itself" in the pursuit of money, sex, and power.

INDIVIDUAL OR GROUP REFLECTION QUESTIONS
1 Explore the ways in which a person with "low self-esteem" may yet be preoccupied with self. Hint: view pride as a spiritual (relational) problem as opposed to a moral one.

2 Consider the contemporary debate on abortion through the lens of "the kingdom of self." Do some movements and leaders fail to take into account the perspective of significant *others?* (father, family, God, etc.) What does this suggest about the ultimate foundation of their position?

3 Indicate several ways in which sinful pride, on one level, may appear to be attractive, as the "real" solution to life's problems, and yet, on another level, leave us frustrated and unfulfilled.

4 In the New Testament Jesus Christ is often depicted as the Lamb of God. In Revelation 5, for instance, the angels of heaven who number thousands upon thousands sing out in a loud voice: "Worthy is the Lamb, who was slain, to receive power and wealth and wisdom and strength and honor and glory and praise!" (Rev. 5:12) Why is it that the Lamb (and not someone else) is worthy to receive power, wealth, wisdom, strength, honor, glory, and praise? What is the author of Revelation trying to communicate with this image? What are the characteristics of the lamb which are being honored? Are these traits which are honored by our culture?

THREE

THE ENSLAVEMENT OF THE SELF:

Money, Sex, and the
Pursuit of Pleasure

T he acts of the sinful nature are obvious: sexual immorality, impurity and debauchery" (Gal. 5:19).

It was a late January morning in 1978. The entire northeastern United States was covered with snow which ranged in height from thirteen inches in Albany, New York to seven inches in parts of Ohio. Harry, who was transporting a load of clothing from New York City to Illinois, was tired of driving the treacherous, nerve-racking roads and so he stopped near Akron, Ohio to get some lunch. However, because he was pressed for time, Harry did something that day which he had never done before. Instead of eating at the truck stop, as was his custom, he decided to buy a sandwich and eat in his truck.

Because it was so cold that day, Harry left the engine of his eighteen wheeler running as he ate. He thought nothing of this since his rig was in the wide open spaces of a truck stop parking lot. Or so he had thought. However, what Harry didn't realize, since he had reentered the cab from the passenger side, was that the left side of his truck was already encased in snow due to the wind and drifts. And though Harry began to eat his sandwich that afternoon, he never finished. His huge body was discovered on the floor of his cab about an hour and a half later by a curious restaurant worker. By evening, the coroner had already determined the cause of death: carbon monoxide. Harry was twenty-nine years old, and he left a wife and three children.

Death by carbon monoxide, as any physician will tell you, is subtle. The gas sneaks up on you, so to speak, replaces the oxygen in your blood, disorients you, mars your judgment, and then it renders you unconscious until death finally takes over. In a similar fashion, the kingdom of self, which we have described in the last chapter, seeps into the life, the very marrow, of a person with remarkable stealth and with devastating effects. Many people don't even realize that it is present. Like carbon monoxide it disorients and confuses; it pollutes judgment, and in the end, it prevents people from seeing their true condition. The one poison leads to physical death; the other to spiritual death.

WESLEY AND KIERKEGAARD ON SPIRITUAL STUPOR

Both John Wesley, the father of Methodism, and Sören Kierkegaard, a nineteenth-century Danish philosopher and theologian, have described, each in his own way, this very dangerous condition of spiritual stupor. The Methodist leader, for instance, in his sermon "The Spirit of Bondage and of Adoption" portrays the "natural man" as one who is in a state of sleep: his spiritual senses are not awake, and the eyes of his understanding are closed.[1] And precisely because the natural man has little understanding of spiritual matters, of the law of God in particular, he is at rest in his ignorance, secure and unmoved in his sin. Simply put, he cannot fear what he does not know. But it is a false security to be sure. "He *sees* not," Wesley writes, "that he stands on the edge of the pit."[2]

However, this condition which Wesley paints is characteristic not only of those who have dulled their spiritual senses through the more despicable sins of lust, drunkenness, or greed, but it is also present in those who boast of their intellect, freedom, and refinement. To use Wesley's own words, "dozed with the opiates of flattery and sin," these people imagine that they walk in great liberty.[3] It is actually a mistaken freedom, however, a freedom not to serve God and neighbor, but only to continue in sin. As a willing, obedient servant of sin, the natural man is not troubled, and he talks, on occasion, of "repenting by and by,"[4] while sin continues its dulling and deadly effects.

Sören Kierkegaard, on the other hand, in his description of the aesthetic stage—which roughly corresponds to Wesley's "natural man"—appears to give the sinner a much more active role in the maintenance of the grand illusion, of life lived as it was never meant to be lived, that is, apart from God. People at this stage, through much effort, try to keep reality and the prospect of eternity and judgment at a distance, and this can be done in a number of ways. They can, for instance, fill their lives with all kinds of pleasure and excitement in order to smother the knowledge that someday they will die. Here expensive cars, opulent homes, or exotic vacations can act like a narcotic drug: they dull spiritual vision as they inflate one's sense of self. Or these "aesthetics" can strive to keep all the options of life open in order to avoid commitment and decision with respect to such things as career, marriage, or personal growth. Here freedom and possibility become idols. Life becomes a fantasy, an illusion. A veneer of pleasure has been placed over the rough edges of human existence with all its seriousness, its meaning and anxiety.

Those who avoid coming to a knowledge of themselves by engaging in such base pleasures as drunkenness, promiscuous sex, and wanton materialism, are in fact suitably described by Kierkegaard's aesthetic stage. It would be a mistake, however, to conclude, once again, that all people at this level of development are in pursuit of "wine, women/men, or song," as the saying goes. Intellectuals, for example, can equally keep reality at bay by constructing mental castles in which they live. Instead of facing forthrightly their own mortality and their spiritual condition, intellectuals can, at times, escape these realities by actually writing lengthy treatises on the subject. By conceptualizing death, by intellectualizing their own mortality, they can conclude that they are done with the matter. However, a professor's (or a sophomore's) twenty-page paper on Kübler-Ross' stages of dying is hardly evidence that the scholar has faced his or her mortality. To be sure, ideas, as well, can keep us from the knowledge of ourselves: we are *existing* beings, not abstract concepts or universal ideas.

In a similar fashion, the gifted poet may give the pain, struggles, and failures of life an artificial cast, a roseate color, that does not ring true. Youth can be glorified, beauty celebrated, and success praised out of all proportion in the meter and rhyme of a language that speaks little of the human condition. As Sontag points out, "Aesthetic presentation always creates a distance between the person and reality, whereas the goal of life is to be immediately involved in the concrete situation."[5]

In this present chapter we shall consider three of the more obvious ways in which the sinful self attempts to hide from itself and from a holy God, looking at ways in which unbelief and pride manifest themselves. Indeed, the allure of money (greed), sex (lust), and pleasure (gluttony) does not simply plague the most rank sinner, but it also entices most of us at least at some point in our spiritual journey.

THE DESIRES OF THE SELF: MONEY, SEX, AND THE PURSUIT OF PLEASURE

Money

In a real sense money represents power, the power to acquire goods and services, to eliminate debts, to finance an education, to pay for a vacation, a car, or some new electronic wizardry. It can guarantee the best medical care available, provide comfortable housing, and offer a means of support in retirement. If used properly, money can bring about great good not only for oneself but for others as well. It can be the wherewithal to feed the hungry, clothe the naked, and house the homeless. Not surprisingly, then, the Bible never states that money is the root of all evil, as it is sometimes incorrectly quoted; rather it affirms, quite simply, "the love of money is a root of all kinds of evil" (1 Tim. 6:10).

One important way in which money can become "a root of all kinds of evil" is when it is deemed intrinsically valuable instead of extrinsically valuable. To illustrate, if something is of intrinsic worth, it is valued for itself and not as a means to some other end. Happiness and the love of God would meet this test, but not many other things would. On the other hand, if something is deemed extrinsically valuable, it is never valued for itself, but is regarded only as *the instrument* or means which will help one to attain what one truly desires.

By now we should be able to see the absurdity of considering money as intrinsically valuable or deeming wealth as an end in itself. Do people, for instance, seek money simply to place it in a room and gaze at it all day long or do they acquire it in order to get the material things which they really desire in life? Indeed, only a truly perverted miser—and there are unfortunately some well-known cases—would ever desire money as an end in itself. Most people seek money not for itself but for what it can do. They see it as a useful instrument to attain what they need and desire.

The real problem, then, with money for most people concerns a misguided instrumental use. Put another way, lacking a sustaining, loving relationship with a holy God who affirms them at their deepest level, men and women often set their hearts on all the various vain things which money can buy. The hope is that these things will bring rich, deep, and lasting happiness and fill the aching void that people sometimes feel inside.

Unfortunately, some people would do most anything for money. And the cynics among us tell us that everyone has his or her price. Take the case of Charles Stuart, for instance. Back in October 1989, the nation was shocked to learn that this young man and his attractive pregnant wife had been robbed at gunpoint and shot. Thinking quickly, Charles Stuart reported the incident on his car phone as the Boston police—and eventually the entire nation—listened to his pleas for help. Though Mr. Stuart recovered from his serious wound, the ambulance had arrived too late to save his wife and their baby.

A few months later, Charles Stuart was well enough to go through the ordeal of identifying a suspect in a police lineup, and he pointed out a young black man as one who resembled the gunman. However, this is when the story began to fall apart. On January 3, 1990, Matthew Stuart, Charles' brother, came forward and told police that Charles had directed him to get rid of a handbag and a .38 caliber revolver around the time of the alleged incident. No doubt pained by his conscience, Matthew confessed to police that he had thrown this damaging evidence in the Pines River, evidence which the police later recovered. The next day, January 4th, Charles Stuart realized the charade was over, and he jumped to his death from a bridge in Boston.

Police investigators later learned that shortly before "the attack" Charles Stuart had taken out several large life insurance policies on his wife. Here was a man, in other words, who wanted to get rich at any cost, even at the expense of his beautiful wife and their unborn baby, even at the expense of the liberty of a young and innocent black man. But what could money buy that Charles Stuart would so desire that he would be willing to sacrifice his own family for it? The nation was not only shocked, but it was now also outraged.

Admittedly, the case of Charles Stuart is an extreme one. Nevertheless, it shows what evil can emerge from the human heart when the desire for riches festers and gets out of control. But lust for wealth does, after all, appear in much more socially acceptable forms. How many Americans, for instance, secretly or openly, envied millionaire Ivan Boesky before his conviction on insider trading on Wall Street? An answer to this question can perhaps be found in the enthusiastic reception that this rich broker received during the 1980s at the University of California at Berkeley when he proclaimed from the podium "the gospel" of our secular age: "There is nothing wrong with greed."

Or how many Americans envied Michael Milken, millionaire and "junk bond king," before he pleaded guilty to six counts of securities fraud in a U.S. district court in New York in 1990? But before we self-righteously pronounce judgment on either Boesky or Milken let us imagine how difficult it might be to maintain personal and spiritual integrity in the face of such enormous power and wealth. Perhaps there are many more Ivan Boeskys and Michael Milkens across the land than we think. In the end, the only difference may be that these unknowns lack the opportunity and the power to fulfill their lusts. This observation does not by any means excuse such behavior, but only tries to understand it.

A much more common way, however, in which middle class men and women fuel their desire for riches is by chasing after the status symbols of American culture in the pursuit of happiness. A few years ago, for instance, one of the big three automakers of Detroit ran an ad campaign that trumpeted the song "If my friends could see me now" as it showed off its latest model of the American dream. More recently, a national cruise line has given new life to this old song in its ads to entice the American public aboard its vacation ships. The point of all this advertising, of course, is to get people to spend money, whether they need the products offered or not. But notice what kind of motivation the writers from Madison Avenue appeal to in these commercials. Simply put, if you buy or use this product, you will be the envy of all your friends (and maybe even of a few of your enemies); therefore, you must be a better person. Nothing could be easier. Self-improvement and an enhanced status in the community can be bought and sold. What a great idea!

But there is, as you probably suspect by now, a downside to all of this. A question which Madison Avenue never addresses in its ad campaigns is what kind of people, in the first place, would seek to improve their status by buying things in order to show off? Are these consumers insecure? Are they content with themselves? Are they trying to ground their personality in things rather than relationships, in having something rather than in being somebody? And do we really want to be like them? Decades ago, Will Rogers, the great American humorist, said it well: "Too many people spend money they haven't earned to buy things they don't want, to impress people they don't like." We do well to heed such wisdom.

But the feverish pursuit of wealth in order to buy happiness, security, or greater respect in the community is not only a personal flaw, it has also become a national obsession. During the "Reagan revolution" in the 1980s, for instance, it became fashionable, once again, to display wealth unapologetically, ostentatiously. From lavish private parties to Nancy Reagan's purchase of new, expensive, and unneeded china for the White House, the message was clear: rich was in. And during his reelection campaign in 1984, Ronald Reagan did not talk much of how his administration would help the poor and the homeless; instead he gloried in the myth of keeping America a place, as he put it, "where anyone can become a millionaire." Again, Reagan's major question along the campaign trail was not "Are *the poor* better off than they were four years ago?" but "Are *you* better off than you were four years ago?" This appeal to crude self-interest, though morally troubling, was politically successful.

One does not have to be a liberal Democrat, however, to realize that Reagan orchestrated a tremendous redistribution of wealth in the United States. Kevin Phillips, a *conservative* analyst, in his book *The Politics of Rich and Poor* demonstrates that during the 1980s wealth did not "trickle down" to the poor as was promised by Arthur Laffer and other point men for the administration; instead, greater wealth was put into the hands of the *already* rich. "No parallel upsurge of riches had been seen," Phillips points out, "since the late nineteenth century, the era of the Vanderbilts, Morgans, and Rockefellers."[6] In fact, the tax cuts of the early 1980s so favored the upper class that by the end of the decade this sector of society had actually increased its already large share of America's goods. Consequently, the top 10 percent of American households now controlled nearly 70 percent of America's net worth.[7]

Again, the 1980s were remarkable in that not only were national politicians celebrating and fostering the very climate which gives rise to greed, envy, and self-absorption, but some of America's leading televangelists were doing much the same—but this time, regrettably, in the name of Jesus. One leading preacher, for instance, heaped praise on the wonders of self-interest and a profit-motivated economic system and then went on to claim that capitalism was both taught and encouraged by the Lord! But how can this be? How can the holy name of Jesus Christ be invoked to justify a modern economic system which leaves the homeless in the streets, the sick untreated, and the hungry unfed? This indictment does not deny that capitalism, with all its faults, is much to be preferred over socialism or Marxism. Nevertheless, have not some televangelists confused the American way of life with the kingdom of God? Christians should wonder.

Even though many sectors of American culture, from politicians to televangelists, encourage one to make more and more money, the pages of the Bible reveal a much different attitude

toward wealth. In the Old Testament, in the Book of Deuteronomy in particular, one of the Ten Commandments warns against
even desiring what your neighbor has: "You shall not covet your
neighbor's wife. You shall not set your desire on your neighbor's
house or land, his manservant or maidservant, his ox or donkey,
or anything that belongs to your neighbor" (Deut. 5:21). The
implication of this commandment, then, is that men and women
are to be content with what they have, that they should be grateful for whatever God has given them. But who teaches such
wisdom today?

The New Testament, moreover, appears to be even more cau-
tious in this area. In the gospels and the epistles, for example, we
find neither encouragement to pursue wealth nor do we find the
attitude that we are entitled to whatever we can acquire. Instead,
we meet caution at every step along the way, indicating that the
potential for evil in this area is great and that the destruction of
the human soul by many hurtful desires may be at stake. Accordingly, Paul advises the troubled Colossian church: "Set your
minds on things above, not on earthly things. . . . Put to death,
therefore, whatever belongs to your earthly nature . . . evil desires and greed, which is idolatry. Because of these, the wrath of
God is coming" (Col. 3:2, 5-6).

How often have we seen greed or covetousness, the desire for
riches, set brother against brother, and sister against sister, as
family members argued over what share of their parents' estate
they ought to inherit. Unfortunately, this is not a new story but
an old one. Just such a situation occurred in the time of Jesus,
and Luke's gospel gives us the troubling details. A man came up
to Jesus and made what he thought was a reasonable request:
"Teacher, tell my brother to divide the inheritance with me"
(Luke 12:13). Clearly, this person thought that he had been treated unfairly by his brother, that his rights had been violated, and
so he approached Jesus as a judge, as one who would give him
justice. His cause was a noble one—or so it seemed—and he
simply wanted his fair share. What could be more simple? What
could be more just? But notice what Jesus did. Instead of encouraging this man, Jesus warned him: "Watch out! Be on your guard
against all kinds of greed; a man's life does not consist in the

abundance of his possessions" (Luke 12:15). The man, no doubt, walked away disappointed.

In fact, in almost every instance where Jesus Christ discussed the subject of money, He issued some kind of stern warning or rebuke. In the Sermon on the Mount, for example, the Master counseled:

> Do not store up for yourselves treasures on earth, where moth and rust destroy, and where thieves break in and steal. But store up for yourselves treasures in heaven where moth and rust do not destroy and where thieves do not break in and steal. For where your treasure is, there your heart will be also" (Matt. 6:19-21).

The last line, however, "For where your treasure is, there your heart will be also," appears to be the key to the whole. Here, Jesus is revealing that riches have a way of placing themselves on the throne of the human heart, a place suitably reserved for God alone. Viewed from another perspective, however, this sin is not only one of alienation from God and idolatry, but one of slavery as well. "No one can serve two masters. Either he will hate the one and love the other, or he will be devoted to the one and despise the other. You cannot serve both God and Money" (Matt. 6:24). In a similar fashion, the author of 1 Timothy writes: "People who want to get rich fall into temptation and a trap and into many foolish and harmful desires. . . . For the love of money is a root of all kinds of evil" (1 Tim. 6:9-10).

Beyond this, riches can create the illusion that the self is sufficient unto itself, that it is independent, that it is not in need of anybody or anything, God included. To be sure, the energetic, driven pursuit of wealth is the stuff of which the kingdom of self is made. Here, the words, "my," "mine," "I," and "self" take on entirely new proportions. The sinful ego inflates itself, feeds itself, with the things of this world. But as those who do not trust in God as the center of their lives attempt to establish their own security through money, they often find that such security, ironically enough, ever escapes them. The richer they become, the more anxious they become. The great fear now, of course, is that they will lose their wealth.

Sex

Sexual desire, in a perverted form, can mimic the desire for money in that it seeks an object, a thing to amuse or enhance a growing sense of self. Here the self is principally a recipient of pleasure, and it basks in the sexual attention shown it. Intimacy, however, is never realized in this "relation" because the self eagerly takes, but it refuses to give. The opposite sex becomes a plaything, a toy, a means of amusement. Indeed, the self in this instance is not at all interested in knowing a person, establishing a relationship, or in pursuing love. It simply wants sex and the pleasure it can bring.

Other sexual desires, though still diverted from their proper course, seem to be an advance over the former in that the self at least seeks some sort of relationship, perhaps realizing, on some level, that the way back to happiness is not through the acquisition of things, but through a loving relationship where the self gives of itself and receives in turn. What's lacking here, however, and what's lacking in much of the sexuality championed in American popular culture the last thirty years is commitment.

During the 1960s, for instance, with contraceptive technology in place, many young people began to engage in sexual relationships more often and more freely than had an earlier generation. Hippies and flower children trooped across the country and staged "love-ins" from Haight Ashbury to Greenwich Village. And two of the more prominent radicals of the era, Abbie Hoffman and Jerry Rubin, called for "free love," that is, love without the benefit of such a "restrictive" commitment as marriage. Moreover, when young people demonstrated against the Vietnam conflict during this era, they chanted "make love, not war." And when they listened to "their" music they heard Steve Stills proclaim the new sexual ethic across the heartland: "Love the one you're with."

The sixties were heady times, to be sure. Conventional morality was shunned, restraints were loosened, and sexual experimentation was in vogue. Sociologists tell us that during times of war, the ethical standards or norms of society are often both challenged and changed. Indeed, it was not long before George and Nena O'Neill actually proposed the novel idea of "open marriage," a relationship in which either partner was "free" to have sex with others. The titillation of the senses, the gratification of the self seemed to be all that mattered. One wondered where it would all end.

Today, many people probably think that the sexual energy of the sixties and seventies has finally evaporated in the more conservative eighties and nineties. After all, the threat of AIDS and of other sexually transmitted diseases like herpes would supposedly put a brake on things. Recent statistics, however, paint a much different picture. A report from the Alan Guttmacher Institute, a research group which is associated with Planned Parenthood, reveals that "more and younger American teenagers had sex in the 1980s than ever before."[8] The report, which was based on a 1988 survey, revealed that 53 percent of teenage girls were sexually active. This figure compares with 47 percent in 1982 and 36 percent in 1973.[9] In addition, a similar report issued by the Urban Institute in 1990 noted that 80 percent of boys had sexual intercourse by the time they reached the age of nineteen.[10] In fact, according to one study, there were more cases of syphilis reported in 1989 "than at any time since 1949."[11] Many of its victims were teenagers.

If the data of the sexual activity of young people today is a cause for alarm — and it is — then so is that of their parents. Adultery appears to be on the rise for both men and women. However, the real surprise here concerns not so much the sexual behavior of men, which has never really been very good, but that of women. Specifically, there are now several reputable studies which suggest that when it comes to infidelity, "women's behavior is definitely becoming more like men's."[12] According to Shere Hite, the controversial author of the book *Women and Love,* infidelity among wives may now be as high as 70 percent.[13] Other researchers, however, disagree. Some therapists and sociologists put the figure around 40 percent — a figure which essentially agrees with a study conducted by *Cosmopolitan* magazine during the early 1980s. But even these figures are hardly cause for encouragement.

Cultural trends are one thing, but what has been the church's role in this ongoing sexual revolution? Some like the leaders of the American Family Association have spoken out forcefully against the pandering to sexual interests which occurs nightly in America's living rooms through national television. On the other hand, some sectors of the church have actually followed these trends, endorsed them, at least to a certain degree, and then dressed them up in religious clothing. In 1987, for example, the Episcopal Church published a 112-page pamphlet entitled *Sexuality: A Divine Gift* which openly questioned "the old rules of sexual abstinence or strict heterosexual monogamy."[14] To add to this moral and spiritual confusion, in 1989 the Episcopal bishop of Newark, John Shelby Spong, published *Living in Sin,* a book which in many respects challenged and renounced the church's historic teaching on human sexuality. According to this liberal bishop, "Sex outside of marriage can be holy and life-giving under some circumstances."[15] Spong's reasoning, though it is very up-to-date, is theologically troubling: "Most people are likely to break the traditional rules anyway," he argues, "what with the advent of birth control and modern life-styles."[16] An appeal to moral failure and self-indulgence are hardly the things of which sound and convincing arguments are made, but it is the stuff of which the kingdom of self is made. The good bishop should have known better.

For those who remain spiritually earnest and who realize the danger of their own self-will in this important area of human sexuality, there is no better resource to consult than the Bible. Bishops and denominational presses may compromise their witness to the sanctity of human sexuality but in the Word of God, at least, we can find a sure and lasting guide to a rich and rewarding spirituality, one which has endured throughout the centuries, which understands the proper goal of human beings, and which, therefore, can offer fulfillment, peace and happiness as men and women practice its wisdom. In fact, the Bible is so rich in detail on this subject of human sexuality that we will have to limit our discussion, for the sake of space, to just two of its major principles.

First of all, the Bible repeatedly warns that human sexuality has proper limits, which if exceeded, will result in anxiety, guilt, and condemnation. The many teachings of Scripture on this topic can be summarized in the one rule that the most intimate human sexual relations are to occur *only* within the context of marriage, that is, within the borders of a committed, lasting relationship. In his letter to the Corinthians, the Apostle Paul explains.

> Do you not know that the wicked will not enter the kingdom of God? Do not be deceived: Neither the sexually immoral nor idolaters nor adulterers nor male prostitutes nor homosexual offenders nor thieves nor the greedy, nor drunkards nor slanderers nor swindlers will inherit the kingdom of God (1 Cor. 6:9-10).

And elsewhere, the author of the Book of Hebrews writes: "Marriage should be honored by all, and the marriage bed kept pure, for God will judge the adulterer and all the sexually immoral" (Heb. 13:4-5).

What the preceding passages mean, then, is that premarital sexual intercourse, living together prior to marriage, affairs by the husband or wife, and lesbian and male homosexual fornication,[17] are all equally rejected and for the same reason: sex outside the marriage bond, outside a holy, covenanted relationship is illicit. To be sure, this sexual ethic is culturally unpopular. The homosexual community, for example, is currently knocking on the doors of the church and is demanding acceptance for its "lifestyle." In fact, some have even championed the recognition of homosexual marriages. However, it must be borne in mind that homosexuality is not an amorphous thing, but is actually made up of a number of sexual practices which many people deem to be immoral. Despite the protests, homosexuality is a moral issue after all. For example, sex outside marriage, which is the staple of homosexuality, as well as the practice of sodomy, anal intercourse in particular, do not elevate and ennoble, instead they degrade and debase the human character.

Moreover, these important ethical and spiritual matters are not to be decided by what is deemed politically correct, nor by a show of hands, but by an appeal to God's Holy Word. Fortunately, in the Bible we find a sexual ethic that can issue in the celebration of deep meaning and of the richest love, unspoiled by either enslaving lust or by selfish rebellion. And if it is true that homosexuals cannot change their sexual *orientation,* though this point is disputed as well, then they are at the very least called to celibacy for the sake of humility and, of course, for holiness.

The second major principle drawn from the Scriptures treats a much different problem, but one no less important. As we have just seen, on the one extreme there are those who maintain that any kind of sexual activity is good so long as there are freely consenting adults involved. But, at the other extreme, there are those within the church who consider *any* sexual activity, even that between a loving husband and wife, as somehow or other infected with sin and therefore as something which ultimately prevents married couples from attaining the very highest spirituality.

For example, many of the Latin church fathers like Tertullian, Ambrose, Jerome, and Augustine, who later influenced Roman Catholicism and to a lesser extent Protestantism, so celebrated virginity that the church eventually came to believe that the richest spiritual life could be enjoyed only by virgins. In fact, it was not really until the time of the Reformation that Martin Luther first seriously challenged this traditional understanding of spirituality and sexuality by leaving the monastery, reentering society, and marrying Katie von Bora.

Now if like Luther and other Reformers, we take guidance preeminently not from church practice or tradition, but from the Word of God itself, a much more balanced and spiritually healthy picture will emerge. In contrast to what many church historians have called a neurotic tradition of sexual repression,[18] both the Old and New Testaments teach that human sexuality is not the principal occasion for evil but is a great good, a gift from the Creator, and within the proper limits, is to be celebrated and enjoyed. Observe the language of Genesis: "God created man in his own image, in the image of God he created him; male and female he created them. God blessed them and said to them, 'Be fruitful and increase in number; fill the earth and subdue it' " (Gen. 1:27-28). Notice in this passage not only that God has created humanity, *male and female,* in His own image, but that He also *commanded* them to "increase in number." Human sexuality and procreation, in other words, cannot be the essence of sin, as is sometimes mistakenly supposed or intimated, but are truly good and honorable. They are nothing less than an expression of the will of God.

Continuing this theme, the author of the Song of Songs actually describes a lover's enjoyment of his beloved with great artistry, sensitivity, and also with remarkably sensuous language. He writes:

How beautiful you are, my darling!
Oh, how beautiful!
Your eyes behind your veil are doves
Your hair is like a flock of goats
descending from Mount Gilead. . . .
Your lips are like a scarlet ribbon;
your mouth is lovely. . . .
Your two breasts are like two fawns,
like twin fawns of a gazelle
that browse among the lilies (Song 4:1, 3, 5).

The remainder of this ancient text portrays sexuality as communion between the lover and the beloved; it suggests the intimacy, abandonment, trust, and surrender which are so much a part of vital spirituality. And it sees the sexual relation as a mirror of still higher things, as an expression of sublime truths and as a window on beauty. In this text, then, God the Redeemer is not at all set against God the Creator.

In his commentary on *The Song of Solomon,* however, Bernard of Clairvaux, a medieval monk, felt compelled to discard the literal sense of this book, with all its sexual overtones, in order to find allegorical meaning. If the literal meaning of the text was unacceptable—because it went against the traditional teaching of the church—then one must explain it away in new meanings. According to Bernard, this book was not about Solomon's love of his wife or human sexuality, but about Christ's love for the church!

In spite of some of the traditional readings of Scripture, it must be reaffirmed that the New Testament, like the Old, offers a healthy and balanced understanding of human sexuality. For example, Paul writes to the Corinthians, "But if you do marry, you have not sinned; and if a virgin marries, she has not sinned" (1 Cor. 7:28). Paul's preference of the single state is not because he views either marriage or sexuality as sinful or as that which necessarily hinders spiritual growth, but because, "those who marry will face many troubles in this life, and I want to spare you this. What I mean, brothers, is that the time is short. . . . For this world in its present form is passing away" (1 Cor. 7:28-29, 31). There is strong evidence, then, in Paul's writings to suggest that he believed the second coming of Christ was imminent and that there was, consequently, no need to marry and to plan for the long-term future.

Moreover, if in contrast to the preceding argument, it is claimed that humanity is now fallen, and therefore all human sexuality is polluted by sinful lust, we respond that the Fall affects not simply our sexual nature, but our entire being. No one sin, therefore, other than unbelief (or possibly pride), should be singled out as the essence of evil. And though no major theologian has ever absolutely equated original sin with human sexuality (not even the once sexually immoral St. Augustine), some theologians nevertheless have left such an implication in their works.

So then, in direct contrast to all those traditions which celebrate virginity as *the way* to spiritual perfection, we will contend in this book that the most rewarding spiritual life, the highest reaches of sanctity, are a possibility for all sorts of people: for housewives, for laity, for over-stressed fathers, for people who work nine-to-five jobs, for active mothers, for college students, and for children, in other words, for anyone who has been created in the image and likeness of God. Though others may protest, the door to the most rewarding spirituality is not shut. Laity and married people are free to enter, drawn and encouraged by the rich grace of God.

THE PURSUIT OF PLEASURE

When we either consciously or unconsciously reject God as the chief "object" of our desires, and thereby place ourselves in the center of things, we often find that there is a tremendous void left in our hearts, that there is yet a deep yearning for something (or someone) better. Consequently, in order to fill this emptiness, we begin to form attachments to pleasure, career, success, physical beauty, or to anything else that will give us a sense of who we are or that will justify our being. In time, however, these attachments may capture our desires, limit them only to particular objects, and thus create a condition of virtual slavery. There are, after all, so many things in the world that can captivate the human heart; there are so many things that can become idols.

Take the case of a middle-aged man whom I met at a Bible study and who was one of the most unhappy persons I had ever encountered. Hal, who was a New York City transit cop at the time, had many reasons to be otherwise: he had a secure job, a beautiful home, a devoted wife, and three overachieving children. And yet he was always either grumpy or argumentative, ever trying to prove his point. On several occasions at the Bible study, for instance, in an attempt to demonstrate his superior knowledge, he corrected the kind and humble minister who was leading the study. The class, however, was not impressed.

It was not long before some of us in the group began to realize what was troubling Hal. Simply put, his real problem was not the Bible study, nor the teacher, nor even the method of instruction, but himself or rather the kingdom of self that he had constructed in the *absence* of a sense of God's gracious love toward him. In Hal's little world, he had already judged himself a failure simply because he lacked a college education. Sadly he then went on to conclude that he was also unworthy of love and esteem. In Hal's mind, at least, one had to be a college graduate or at least appear intelligent in order to be loved. However, by making a god out of intellect, by becoming attached to such a limited understanding of self-worth, Hal not only tormented others, but himself as well.

Though Hal aimed at the appearance of intelligence as the chief good of his life, many people simply aim at pleasure, sometimes in some very raw forms. Here the purpose of life is to enjoy life, to be entertained, to have fun, to stimulate the senses, and to eliminate pain and suffering at every opportunity. "Life's a beach," "Life's a party" — or so we are told. Indeed, ask many people what is the purpose of life and they will tell you it is to be happy. Press them further and you will discover that, for quite a few of them, happiness *equals* pleasure.

But does the pursuit of pleasure always bring happiness? It depends on what you mean by these terms. If pleasure means an enjoyable stimulation of the senses, and happiness means a sense of serenity, integrity, and fulfillment which is not subject to changing circumstances, then it must be concluded that not all pleasure brings happiness. First of all, there are those pleasures which only last for a season. A woman, for instance, may take pride in her physical attractiveness, only to watch this pleasure slip away as she ages. A man may enjoy watching the stock market each day, only to become depressed when it falls. Or a teenager may delight in gossiping about another, only to find that no one confides in her any longer and that she has actually become unpopular. Notice that in each instance, the desire of our heart eventually fails; what we counted on to give us pleasure, satisfaction, and meaning, no longer works. In light of these dynamics, we must be very careful about what we desire and what we set our heart on, for the prospect of frustration, pain, and disappointment is great.

Second, what happens when our attachment to sensual pleasures not only replaces our desire for God, but also becomes outright addictive? What is to be done when we no longer have the freedom *not* to be competitive, when we no longer can stay away from a mirror, a drink, or a drug, or a destructive relationship, when our sense of self is so tied up in these things that we can no longer escape? Put another way, what can we do in the face of radical evil, when our lives are on the line, so to speak?

Take the case of a young man who was a member of a church which I attended a few years ago. Phil, a very likable fellow, had his first drink when he was fifteen years old. Like most of his friends, he drank throughout high school, often before entering one of his school's many social functions. When he went off to college a few years later he continued to drink, though, of course, less secretly. At this time, however, alcohol was not really a problem for him. It was fun and he enjoyed its effects. "It calmed me down and helped me to overcome my shyness," he said.

After college, Phil, who had always been bright, entered a prestigious law school. Interestingly enough, this "success" was to be the beginning of his troubles. As an undergraduate, Phil had become used to being recognized as one of the brightest in his class and he fed on this pleasure. It soon became a part of his own self-perception. In law school, however, with so many intelligent people in his class, Phil was now just "average." He felt lost. The pattern of behavior which had given him so much pleasure and which had supported him so well in the past no longer worked. The king had been dethroned; his idols fell to the floor. What was Phil to do? After assessing the situation, he anxiously decided to redouble his efforts, to work at the maximum of his potential: he studied harder and longer; he attended every class; and he became much more competitive. And why not? As Phil later told me "his life was at stake." And in a sense it was.

It was also about this time when Phil began to have trouble with his drinking. Alcohol was now functioning as a drug for him, as a release valve to wash away the petty frustrations, setbacks, and indignities of law school. And it worked—at least for awhile. But in time Phil began to notice that he was having "blackouts," memory losses as a result of drunkenness. People would come up to him and question him about his behavior the night before, but he would hardly remember a thing; it was all a blur. Phil continued his self-destructive cycle of resentment, drinking, and blackouts until finally he dropped out of law school. He is still struggling with alcohol today.

Sadly enough, Phil's case is not an uncommon one. According to recent statistics, in the United States today "approximately 22 million Americans, one out of seven, are drinking alcoholically."[19] Obviously, these are not all skid row bums. Contrary to some popular myths, alcoholism is found in every socio-economic class, among the rich as well as among the poor. It strikes young people, old people, blacks, whites, reds, yellows, Gentiles, Jews, women, men, religious people, atheists, athletes, musicians, stock brokers—and law students. In fact, if you are a doctor, dentist, pharmacist, or nurse, your chance of succumbing to alcoholism is thirty-five times higher than the rate among the general population.[20] So much for skid row bums.

One of the first steps in combating alcoholism—and other addictions—is to dispel the ignorance which surrounds it. Some people think, for instance, especially within the walls of the church, that alcoholism is basically a moral problem, that if the person just exercised more willpower he or she could stop drinking. Their response, in other words, to this physical, emotional, and spiritual problem is some form of moralism. They think that if only the person would attend church more often, "get involved" in committee work and social projects, the problem would take care of itself. Once the level of addiction is reached, however, alcoholics are unable *by themselves* to break the chains of repeated use which hold them in place. Simply put, the self by itself is unable to recover.

Viewed from the vantage point of spirituality, which considers the depths of the human heart and its relationship to a transcendent God, the problem of alcoholism (as with other forms of addictive pleasure) appears to be that the will has been corrupted as described by St. Paul: "For in my inner being I delight in God's law; but I see another law at work in the members of my body, waging war against the law of my mind and making me a prisoner of the law of sin at work within my members" (Rom. 7:22-23). Caught up in the whirlwind of a divided will (one part of the personality wants to stop; the other part doesn't) alcoholics no longer enjoy the liberty of not drinking through their own efforts. In other words, self-will cannot free itself from the shackles of addiction precisely because the shackles are *within* self-will. This is what moralism ever fails to understand.

Having encountered radical evil, an evil which left untreated will destroy them, alcoholics need nothing less than the powerful grace of Almighty God, nothing less than a spirituality which will get them beyond themselves (and their corrupted, divided wills) to enjoy fellowship with the Most High. Moralizing from the pulpit will not do. Pious platitudes will not work. And though we have focused on alcoholism as one example of pleasure-seeking gone wrong, many other "pleasures" will demonstrate the same dynamics, whether it be vanity, addiction to competition, bulimia, cigarette smoking, or sexual promiscuity.

To be sure, addiction to various pleasures is destructive; nevertheless, and oddly enough, great good can come out of this. When I was a chaplain at a college in the South a few years ago, my own spiritual counseling with teenage alcoholics convinced me that some of these young people had wisdom far beyond their age. They at least knew, if their elders did not, that the kingdom of self is bankrupt, that the pursuit of pleasure is empty, that attempts at self-improvement never go far enough, and that self-will can be the greatest slavery of all. No doubt humbled by their experiences and knowing their need, these boys and girls were ready to try something which the self-righteous always reject: that is, to live under the gracious rule of God, to submit their will to a sovereign Lord. Jesus expressed this dynamic well: "I tell you the truth, the tax collectors and the prostitutes are entering the kingdom of God ahead of you" (Matt. 21:31). Out of pain, then, can come great hope; out of suffering can come healing. God's love, grace, and power will bring wholeness. Spirituality will point the way.

SUMMING UP

In this chapter we have explored how money, sex, and the pursuit of pleasure can have a narcotic effect such that the self is left virtually unaware of its true condition: its isolation and alienation from the fount of deep and abiding meaning, namely, a God of love.

Beyond this, we have considered how the sinful self (since it is independent of God) seeks to secure and strengthen its central position in life by "enlarging" itself through acquiring things, seeking a variety of sexual experiences, and by pursuing pleasure. Though in the short term this strategy appears to work, so effective is the delusion, in the long run, it will leave in its wake anxiety, emptiness, and possibly outright addiction.

On the other hand, in the following chapter, we will examine the conflict which inevitably emerges when one kingdom of self encounters another. The responses of a "monarch" whose rule is challenged by others will be ambition, envy, strife, and anger — the ingredients not for happiness and peace, but for the creation of a living hell.

INDIVIDUAL OR GROUP REFLECTION QUESTIONS

1 Explore some of the ways in which American society celebrates wealth. What kind of values are being promoted here? What is the impact of all of this on spirituality?

2 If you were a friend of Hal's, what would you do to help him? How could you break through all the defense mechanisms (e.g., pride, arrogance) which he has set up to protect his personality? Would talking of the deep humility of Jesus be helpful? If so, how so? If not, why not?

3 Discuss with your friends some of the things in the past on which you have set your heart. Was there any suffering or disappointment associated with these desires? Why? Moreover, what have you learned from these experiences in terms of God and yourself?

4 Gerald May in his book *Grace and Addiction* indicates that many of us are addicted to all sorts of things which can include the following:

> Being attractive, candy, chocolate, coffee, competition, computers, contests, drinking, drugs, eating, exercise, fantasies, fishing, gambling, golf, gossiping, money, seductiveness, sleeping, the stock market, talking, tobacco, and winning.[21]

Why is spirituality in the twofold sense of an honest acknowledgment of our own evil as well as submission to God often necessary in order to overcome many of these addictive behaviors? Why can't the self solve its own problems without God? What are the implications of this important truth?

FOUR

THE SELF THREATENED:
Ambition, Envy, Strife, and Anger

The acts of the sinful nature are obvious . . . hatred, discord, jealousy, fits of rage, selfish ambition, dissensions, factions and envy" (Gal. 5:19-21).

When men and women, for whatever reason, refuse to acknowledge their dependence on God, when they put aside the knowledge that they are, after all, creatures and not the source of life, they are left with a truly impossible task; namely, to establish themselves, to make themselves secure apart from God. Like the prodigal son of Luke's gospel, though they already have everything at their father's house which could make them happy, strangely enough, they set out on their own to find their way in a world of tempting possibilities.

It will not take long, however, before some honest and perceptive men and women will begin to realize that the human condition is fraught with the very ingredients which make for insecurity. Death, disease, misfortune, guilt, and anxiety come to all of us and sometimes when it is least expected. Jim Fixx, for example, the author of *The Complete Book of Running*, had no idea that his afternoon run on July 20, 1984 was to be his last. Nor did Senator John Heinz of Pennsylvania, the heir to the H.J. Heinz fortune, realize that on April 4, 1991 his private jet would collide with a helicopter killing all five persons aboard the two craft as well as two children in a school play yard. These and similar tragedies can happen to any one of us. We are, after all, not so different from one another. The old saying is true: "Here today; gone tomorrow."

However, for those who choose to remain apart from God, there are two key ways by which they can respond to life's insecurity. On the one hand they can, like the existentialist philosophers before them (Nietzsche, Sartre, Camus), assert that life is basically absurd and, therefore, lacks ultimate meaning. It is "a tale told by an idiot, full of sound and fury, signifying nothing."[1] Here human life becomes, in the fashion of Nietzsche's superman (*ubermensch*), a heroic struggle against the void, a herculean conflict against the abyss of meaninglessness. However, how many individuals have the courage to be a superman, to be content with the very small consolations which are wrested from an absurd existence? Not many, to be sure.

On the other hand, a much more popular way of coping with the human condition is to ignore, in a determined fashion, the limitations of human creatureliness like death, guilt, and meaninglessness, and to attempt to overcome basic human insecurity through a raw will to power. Interestingly, there are two key elements in this approach. First, there is an element of self-deception. People *pretend* that they are not limited; they feign that they are independent, self-sufficient. Indeed, this is an illusion which is often tightly (and neurotically) held in the face of much contradictory evidence. Second, there is an element of self-assertion. Thus, with lingering insecurity in place, the self attempts to satisfy its basic security needs by promoting itself, by calculating self-interest at every opportunity, and by grabbing an ever larger portion of life's offerings, even at the expense of others. And though this strategy of putting the ego at the center of existence appears, at first glance, to issue in more security for the individual, over time it actually produces less, much less, as will be apparent shortly.

In the last chapter we demonstrated the many ways in which people seek to preoccupy themselves and avoid the larger issues of life: by acquiring more money, engaging in illicit sexual relations, and pursuing pleasure for its own sake. Indeed, if we were to sum up the basic perspective of the previous chapter it would be some form of the verb "to have." Simply put, acquiring (broadly understood) is life; owning is existence. And though the perspective of this present chapter can also be described by the verb "to have," a much better choice can be found in the verb "to do." Not owning but doing, not acquiring but achieving, not wealth, but human respect will be the chief terms here.

AMBITION: ANOTHER NAME FOR THE WILL TO POWER

It was Vince Lombardi who led the Green Bay Packers to the first ever Super Bowl championship in 1967 who coined the phrase, "Winning isn't everything; it's the only thing." Few people, however, are actually willing to be so honest about their own ambition, about the pursuit of success or winning at any cost. Sallust (Gaius Sallustius Crispus) the Roman historian expressed it well: "Ambition [drives] many men to become false; to have one thought locked in the breast, another ready on the tongue." To be sure, many men and women tend to hide their ambition out of a sense of shame and therefore cloak their vigorous pursuit of power or honor in various ways.

First of all, there are those people who are so hungry for the praise and approval of their peers that they use an ingenious but deceptive "reverse strategy" to get what they want. These men and women constantly and unnecessarily belittle their own efforts and achievements precisely in order that others may correct them and in turn heap lavish praise on them. But there's a downside to all of this. It's a strategy that works only for awhile. Eventually many catch on and refuse to participate in the charade.

A second and much more common strategy involves deceiving both oneself and others as to the real intent of one's actions. Specifically, it involves draping the noble banner of "the pursuit of excellence" over what is otherwise called mean, selfish ambition. So understood, men and women are not really attempting to improve their own position at the expense of others; they are simply trying to be the best that they can be; they want, after all, to develop *all* of their God-given talents. And if the virtues of discipline and hard work lead to their advancement over others, so be it. It is a happy though unintended side effect. But is it really? And though many take comfort in the thought "I compete with myself, but not with others," they fail to realize that competition always involves more than one.

One of the many problems with sinful ambition is that it appears to be so noble. What could possibly be wrong with self-improvement, with developing one's gifts, graces, and talents? Interestingly enough, sinful ambition is a temptation for the sincere and earnest among us, not for the lazy. Indeed, those who fall under its sway look down on the "wine, women/men, and song" types of the last chapter as wasteful underachievers. Nevertheless, sinful ambition takes what is basically good, namely, the desire to improve oneself, and perverts it by turning it into yet another form of self-absorption. It is a vice which masquerades as a virtue.

The World of Literature

A classic example of obsessive ambition is found in the writings of F. Scott Fitzgerald. In his novel, *The Great Gatsby,* which first appeared in 1925, Fitzgerald details the life of Jay Gatsby, the son of poor parents from the Midwest, who tries to make it in what he perceives as the more socially acceptable society of a wealthy Long Island suburb. The young, nearly penniless Gatsby fails to win the affection of the flirtatious Daisy who prefers to marry the rich and influential Tom Buchanan. Shortly before the wedding, however, Daisy receives a letter—obviously from Gatsby—gets drunk, and sobs that she has changed her mind. After she becomes sober, however, Daisy proceeds with the wedding as planned.

The novel hinges on Jay Gatsby's ambitious attempts to become rich and powerful in order to impress the now married Daisy and to win her back. And Gatsby is greatly encouraged in all this when he realizes that Daisy is unhappy in her marriage. With a plan in mind, Gatsby has his friend Nick Carraway, the narrator of the story, arrange a social tea so that he can meet Daisy. The meeting itself does not go well, though Gatsby recovers by inviting Daisy over to his mansion. Here Gatsby is in his element. The mansion itself, its lavish furniture, the swimming pool, the neatly arranged gardens, as well as Gatsby's expensive clothes, all form the backdrop of his attempt to woo Daisy and to overcome his past romantic failure. Though the manner in which Gatsby acquired his money is suspicious, financial success, the heart of the American dream and the spirit of the Jazz Age, was supposed to transform Daisy into a compliant, adoring lover. But it didn't work. As an English saint once remarked: "A man thinks that many are praising him, and talking of him alone, and yet they spend but a very small part of the day thinking of him, being occupied with things of their own."[2]

Though Jay Gatsby is rich, hard-working, and sincere in his love of Daisy, he is nevertheless a pathetic figure. His driven desire to be a success, at most any cost, inevitably prevents him from coming to a real, lasting knowledge of himself. Clearly, Jay Gatsby never questions who he is in a sensitive and probing way. Like all too many people, he is content with defining himself in terms of the likes and dislikes of others which fluctuate like the wind, and in terms of the idols strewn across the American landscape. The scene of Gatsby lonely in his mansion, surrounded by the trappings of success, suggests that all his wealth, the fruit of his ambition, is a veneer under which lies a sad, troubled, and unknown man. Ambition is like that. It leaves an external shell, but destroys all that is within.

The Bible

Perhaps the most convincing evidence that the temptation to sinful ambition touches the finest among us is found in the pages of the Bible. In the gospel of Luke, for example, we learn that even Jesus Christ faced this temptation just before embarking on His public ministry. Luke writes:

> The devil led him [Jesus] up to a high place and showed him in an instant all the kingdoms of the world. And he said to him, "I will give you all their authority and splendor, for it has been given to me, and I can give it to anyone I want to. So if you worship me, it will all be yours. Jesus answered, "It is written: 'Worship the Lord your God and serve him only' " (Luke 4:5-8).

Notice how the devil in this passage tries to allure Christ with the vain pomp and splendor of this world. Notice also how Satan claims that all of this fleeting authority has been handed over to him and thus he may dispense the spoils as he wills. But Jesus refuses to succumb to any self-serving, grandiose designs of power at the expense of obedience to the Father. "Worship the Lord your God and serve him only," He replies. Jesus was tempted like us in every way, but He was without sin.

Where Jesus succeeded, however, the apostles failed; where Jesus was submissive, the apostles were assertive; where Jesus was humble, the disciples were proud. Mark, for example, writes of the sharp contrast between Christ and His disciples:

> They came to Capernaum. When he [Jesus] was in the house he asked them, "What were you arguing about on the road?" But they kept quiet because on the way they had argued about who was the greatest.
>
> Sitting down, Jesus called the Twelve; and said, "If anyone wants to be first, he must be the very last, and the servant of all."
>
> He took a little child and had him stand among them. Taking him in his arms, he said to them, "Whoever welcomes one of these little children in my name welcomes me; and whoever welcomes me does not welcome me but the one who sent me" (Mark 9:33-37).

What is truly ironic about this account is that the disciples discussed who among them is the greatest immediately after Jesus had just given them a very clear prediction of what awaited Him in Jerusalem — suffering and an ignominious death. Jesus talked of suffering; the disciples talked of power. Jesus spoke of sacrifice; the disciples spoke of self-glory. Yet on some level in their hearts the disciples knew that they were wrong, for when Jesus asked them what they had been arguing about along the way they had nothing to say. Jesus, however, sat them down and in a very pastoral fashion told the disciples something marvelous: that if they sought after true greatness in His kingdom they must find it, not by being first but by being last, not by being proud but by being humble, not by glorifying self, but by glorifying God.

In a similar fashion in a later passage, Mark underscores the striving and selfish ambition of some of the disciples. But this time the culprits are not all the disciples, as in the previous account, but only the Zebedee brothers. Mark explains:

> Then James and John, the sons of Zebedee, came to him. "Teacher," they said, "we want you to do for us whatever we ask."
>
> "What do you want me to do for you?" he asked.
>
> They replied, "Let one of us sit at your right and the other at your left, in your glory."
>
> "You don't know what you are asking," Jesus said. "Can you drink the cup I drink or be baptized with the baptism I am baptized with?"
>
> "We can," they answered.
>
> Jesus said to them, "You will drink the cup I drink and be baptized with the baptism I am baptized with, but to sit at my right or left is not for me to grant. These places belong to those for whom they have been prepared."
>
> When the ten heard about this, they became indignant with James and John (Mark 10:35-41).

It is one thing to aim at honor as an end in itself; it is quite another thing, however, to aim at the things that make for honor. When Jesus was to enter His glory, as King of Kings and Lord of Lords, James and John wanted to make sure that they, and they alone, would be next in line, second in command, the heirs to rule and privilege. James and John, at least at this point in their ministry, were acting like so many of the driven men and women of our own age who strive to climb the corporate ladder or who seek to become upwardly mobile. James and John dreamed of power, honor, and glory, and their plans did not include the other disciples. In this they were little different from the masses of contemporary humanity who are more than eager to advance at the expense of others. The actions of Jesus, on the other hand, were quite uncommon and remarkable. He spoke not of self-interest but of service and of His own sacrifice which lay ahead.

These two scenes from the gospel of Mark, then, have shown us a good deal about the disciples, how human they were, how slow they were to understand spiritual matters, and how self-absorbed they could be. Though they were the disciples of Jesus, they didn't yet understand the meaning of the kingdom of God, nor had they yet tasted of its peace and joy. They still thought like children of the world and not like children of the Most High. Indeed, it would take the reality of a blood-spattered cross to rid James and John as well as the other disciples of their misguided notions concerning the kingdom of God.

THE FRUIT OF AMBITION: ENVY, STRIFE, AND ANGER

Envy

What some ambitious men and women fail to realize is that along the path to "success" are not only many obstacles to be overcome, but also many people who are outright envious of their good fortune. Indeed, to stand out from the crowd, to distinguish oneself, even in some very noble ways, is to invite attack from envious others. For every person who is compassionate toward us in times of trouble, there are perhaps a hundred who sincerely envy our success.

Like ambition, envy is often very subtle and it strikes the best of us. Oscar Wilde once told a fictional story which illustrates this truth. The devil was crossing the Libyan desert, and he came across a group of demons who were tempting a holy monk. These evil spirits pestered the holy man with temptations of the flesh, and they tried to break his faith by sowing both doubt and fear in his soul. Failing in this, they told him that his ascetic practices were all but worthless. But the monk was unmoved. The devil then stepped forward and berated the demons for their primitive methods. He turned to the monk and whispered in his ear, "Have you heard the news? Your brother has just been made the bishop of Alexandria." A grimace of envy descended on the face of the once holy man; he had finally succumbed.

Though envy strikes the best of us, one of its truly remarkable characteristics is that it seldom crosses professional lines.[3] Thus, we are more likely to be envious of those who just outstrip us in our own area of competence than of any others: the accountant is envious of a fellow accountant, a lawyer of a fellow lawyer, a writer of another writer. Take the case of Leonardo da Vinci, gifted artist, scientist, and inventor. During the early part of the sixteenth century, when Leonardo was quite old, he was approached by the rulers of Florence and asked to submit some drawings for the decoration of the grand hall at Florence. Michelangelo, little known at the time, was also asked to submit sketches. The leaders of Florence viewed the work of Leonardo and were, of course, greatly impressed. However, when they considered the artistry of young Michelangelo they were astonished at his bold creativity and imagination. And it is reported that when Leonardo learned of the judgment of the city leaders he became sullen and was never really able to recover. His glory, which he greatly cherished, had been eclipsed by another.

As this story amply illustrates the elder can, at times, envy the younger. But, interestingly enough, the reverse is seldom the case. Young men and women, for instance, can hear their colleagues from another generation praised out of all sense of proportion without feeling the slightest twinge of envy. This is probably only because the young can still take comfort in the notion — vain as it is — that they have not yet had sufficient time to develop all of their gifts, graces, and talents and that given the right opportunity, they too will have their day in the sun.

At any rate, every generation, both young and old alike, back to the dawn of humanity has realized that the life blood of envy is comparison, the tendency to judge ourselves in relation to others. If, however, we constantly compare ourselves to others, and if we continually define our sense of self-worth in terms of how our neighbors are doing, we are programmed for failure and disappointment and in the end unhappiness. Put another way, the spirit of envy creates an illusory world in our hearts, a world that can never be, indeed should never be, a world in which the self, not God, is at the center of things. Accordingly, every success of our neighbor is like a wound; every advancement another blow. Envy causes pain where there should be joy. Dryden called it nothing less than "the jaundice of the soul."

At its root, envy is informed by both unbelief and fear. Forgetting or perhaps denying outright our relationship to God, we now fear that the love given to others necessarily means that we will be loved less. Rejecting our "vertical" relationship with God, we are left only with the ebb and flow of "horizontal" relationships. Consequently, we are now subject, in a powerful way, to the whims and opinions of others. We have become, in effect, a slave to the applause of the crowd.

Out of this same fear of not being loved arises not only envy of other people, but also the appalling attempt to demean or belittle them in the eyes of others, to bring them down to size, so to speak, to do all that we can to make sure that they never advance beyond us. W.E. Sangster, the popular British Methodist preacher, understood these dynamics well and wrote on one occasion:

> It was jealousy that took the heart out of the congratulations you felt obliged to give, that kept you silent when you heard him unfairly criticized, that made you secretly glad when he stumbled and fell. It was jealousy, petty loathsome jealousy, the jealousy which, at its worst, can be incredibly cruel.[4]

Fortunately, there are a number of antidotes to this sickness of soul, among which we must include a humble and thoroughgoing appreciation for all the blessings which we do, in fact, have. Truly, it is difficult, if not impossible, to be envious of another so long as we walk in a spirit of gratitude. But so many elements in our modern North American culture pull us in a much different direction, not toward contentment and peace, but toward dissatisfaction and pain. In fact, the advertising executives on Madison Avenue have made a science of creating discontent and of fostering new, artificial wants in the American people so that they will then turn around and consume more and more. A spirit of appreciation or contentment, no doubt, will all but ruin sales. The ads, therefore, must create a need and stroke desire in order to be successful.

Another antidote to the spirit of jealousy consists in the frank recognition that we see only part of the picture. That is, behind public success there may be private pain; behind the joyous applause of the crowd, there may be hidden sorrow. We really know little of the emotional torment and the repeated failures which may lurk behind personal achievement. Abraham Lincoln, for instance, may have been the envy of his age when he first rose to the office of the presidency. However, for those in the nineteenth century who were well-acquainted with the details of this president's life, his numerous setbacks and political struggles, his wife's mental illness, and his own bouts of depression, envy was hardly possible. Envy thrives in darkness and ignorance. The light of knowledge, however, will sometimes dissipate it.

Strife

If people are committed to their own self-interest, even to the detriment of others, if they pursue their own advantage at most any cost, this is a prescription for disaster. Indeed, those who have set up the kingdom of self are unwilling to tolerate other "monarchs." They themselves must rule—or else. However, many others have enthroned themselves just as the "king and queen makers" have done. Accordingly, conflict, dissension, and chaos are inevitably left in the wake of the frenzied struggle for preeminence. Add to this competing self-interest the jealousy which it inevitably spawns and we have all the ingredients necessary to create a real personal (or public) hell. Not everyone can be number one, nor can all be kings or queens. The letter of James cautions:

> But if you harbor bitter envy and selfish ambition in your hearts, do not boast about it or deny the truth. Such "wisdom" does not come down from heaven but is earthly, unspiritual, of the devil. For where you have envy and selfish ambition, there you find disorder and every evil practice (James 3:14-16).

A recent and sad example of ambition gone wrong, one which angered many athletes and, no doubt, caused much resentment, was displayed for all the world to see at the summer Olympic games held in Seoul, South Korea in 1988. Ben Johnson, an athlete from Canada, rocketed across the finish line of the men's 100-meter race. His official time not only set a new Olympic record, but a world record as well. But, in the end, the honor was stripped from this athlete and given to another, the American Carl Lewis. It was later determined by officials that Johnson had cheated in order to win. Traces of steroids, a drug which enhances muscular strength, were found in his body.

Oddly enough, a far more serious instance of destructive competitiveness which produced strife, anger, and disappointment occurred not at a world-class athletic event, but at a competition for a spot on a cheerleading squad! A woman from Channelview, Texas was convicted by a district court of attempting to hire a gunman to kill the mother of one of her daughter's classmates. It appears that both daughters were contending for a much-desired position as a cheerleader. Prosecutors alleged that the woman hoped that the emotional trauma of coping with her mother's death would effectively eliminate her daughter's rival from the competition. Apparently, the indicted woman was so focused on her goal of seeing her daughter succeed, that she gave little consideration to the rights and feelings of the family of her daughter's rival and to the lifelong consequences which would result from her actions.

Though few of us have met the likes of this driven woman, each one of us knows what it is like to be around extremely competitive people. Our discomfort in their presence naturally grows out of the expectation (and fear) that we will be judged— and found wanting—and that in the end there will be bickering, strife, and hurt feelings. Who likes to be around people who constantly talk about themselves, who brag and boast on most every occasion? Who likes to associate with the insincere who flatter the powerful for advantage only to curse them behind their backs? Truly, the self-centeredness of competitive people can rend the social fabric and disrupt personal relationships. Arguments can be "won," but friendships lost; people can insist they're right, though their hearts are wrong; and those who know it all, know nothing as they should.

In the classroom setting, for instance, there are always one or two people who are keenly interested in everybody else's grades, and of course they will be more than happy to tell you of their own better scores. It seems that these people cannot be happy unless they know that they are "better" than everybody else. They must be king (or queen) of the hill. Nothing less will do; anything else will create dreadful anxiety. In fact, their insecurity runs so deep, their fear and alienation is so disturbing, that they actually feed on the failure of others to enhance their own sense of self-worth. And it is this behavior, in conjunction with others, which causes great discord and much strife in any sort of social group, whether it be at work or at play. Pretending to be God, by placing oneself at the center of existence, can never lead to deep, rich, and lasting happiness. Nor can it lead to peace.

Anger

Up to this point we have been assuming that the ambitious can be largely successful in their efforts, that if enough drive and will-power are expended, they can achieve whatever they want. But this is certainly not always the case. Do what they may, the ambitious—as with everyone else—will eventually experience defeat, rejection, and disappointment. Reality, painful at times, will inevitably break through the illusion that the ego can march from one success story to another. Reality, at some point, will whisper in the ear of all the ambitious, "No!"

This "No" of defeat and rejection can come in many forms. It can take the shape of another competitor who wins "the prize" or of a prize that is withdrawn. It can arise as a set of circumstances beyond the control of the ambitious which frustrates their every design or it can emerge as a result of their own inadequacy. Whatever the source, those who have not yet fully realized how much greater life is than they are will attempt to meet this "loss of control" with anger and with redoubled efforts. They will strike out, fulminate, and storm. But it will all be pointless.

Under such conditions anger represents, on one level, congealed self-will. The petty monarch which has set itself up has found something that will not obey its desire for enlargement and so it responds in anger as if to say, "How dare you oppose my rule, how dare you oppose my advancement!" Put another way, the circumstances of life have been bold enough to transgress the laws and authority of the kingdom of self. Undoubtedly in its protest, the self will portray its cause as a noble one. It will studiously neglect self-examination and will externalize its failure by blaming people, circumstances, or things. It will cry injustice in the most righteous tones, and it will discourse on right and wrong at length. But observe that such moral language is never defined beyond the circle of self—this is a parameter beyond which it will not go. Lord Halifax said it well, "Anger is seldom without argument but seldom with a good one."

This is not to suggest, however, that all anger is sinful. We can, after all, be justifiably angry when the difference is great between actual practice and what is deemed just. For the most part, however, justifiable anger concerns not so much the welfare of ourselves but that of *others* as when Jesus cleansed the temple because the money changers had, first of all, dishonored God by turning the Jerusalem temple into a marketplace and secondly because they had fleeced the worshipers. Indeed, we will search the Bible in vain for a single instance of the anger of Jesus that was an expression of His own self-interest. Bonhoeffer, then, was certainly correct when he wrote that Jesus was "the man for others."

There is yet another form which anger can take: one which is more subtle and less hot and fiery. Indeed, resentment seldom bursts forth like anger nor is it as animated; instead it slowly works its way into the human heart and robs it of both peace and joy. It can simmer for weeks, months, and in some cases, even years. As the etymology of the word suggests (from the French verb *sentir)*, resentment involves a re-feeling of pain. It is a rehashing of old hurts, an opening up of old wounds. Like anger, its power to harm the soul is held in place by a keen sense of injustice, a well-developed sense of right and wrong—elements which make it appear righteous. To be sure, resentment often embodies the indignation felt as a result not of some imagined wrong, but of a very real one. And this is precisely why it is so difficult to be free of its power.

And so here is an irony which all those who want to be liberated from the dominion of evil in their lives must face: though injustice has been done, though people have truly wronged us in the past, for the sake of our own serenity and also for a renewed sense of gratitude, we must let all of these things go. We must, in other words, find a way to transcend our hurt and pain in order to forgive; we must find a way to love those who appear to be unlovable. This does not mean, however, that we will no longer be concerned with issues of justice; it simply means that those issues will now be considered within the larger circle of love. And, of course, we always do well to consider our own sense of being wronged, for the sake of proportion, against the backdrop of the injustices done to Jesus Christ. As one writer put it, "nothing that ever happened in this universe was more unrighteous than the Cross . . . [and yet] they did not crucify an angry man."[5]

Precisely because life is not set up to sustain the petty fiefdoms of the overly ambitious, there is hope. Clearly, the illusion of being at the center of things is dispelled, given enough time, by failure, disappointment, and by the opposition of others. Deep in their hearts, godplayers,[6] those who make themselves number one in life, know that they cannot continue to live the same old way. Alienation from the human community and from God, the source of all life, and even from themselves naturally produces great suffering—a suffering which, however, can prove to be both illuminating and remarkably healing.

More to the point, this process of growth, pain, and greater self-awareness calls for a rethinking of the role of suffering in our lives. In many respects, modern American culture teaches us that suffering is most often bad, a negative thing to be avoided whenever possible. If you are in pain, take a drug; if you are in an unhappy marital relationship, leave it. Though there is pain which is needless and senseless (and we're not talking about that), some physical pain or suffering is actually beneficial as any good doctor knows. It's a warning light that lets us know that something is wrong. Regardless of what we are doing, physical pain will always get our attention; its message is that important.

In the same way, the emotional or spiritual pain caused by selfish ambition, envy, or anger can be a good indication that something is terribly wrong with our way of living. Life can easily become confused, stressful, and chaotic because of a misplaced center. Moreover, when ambitious men and women realize that their own actions have led to strife and discord in their families or on the job, when they feel the pain of rejection by former friends, or when they labor under the continual criticism of colleagues, this is a good sign, painful though it is, that changes are in order. However, strange as it may seem, one of the last persons to realize that he or she has an "I" problem is the person who has it. Self-deception is often that good.

The author who perhaps best describes the transforming and redemptive power of suffering is Fyodor Dostoyevski, the great Russian novelist. In *The Brothers Karamazov,* for instance, written in the latter part of the nineteenth century, Dostoyevski displays the conversion which occurs in the life of Dmitri Karamazov as he learns the lessons of deep but meaningful suffering. At the outset, Dmitri is both passionate and greedy, ever concerned about his inheritance and what his father, Fyodor, can do for him. But by the end of the novel, Dmitri has been transformed by suffering to become a sensitive and caring man who practices love and who takes to heart the counsel of the saintly Father Zossima. One of the more important themes of this work is the revelation that Dmitri's transformation would have been impossible without suffering. Nothing else, perhaps, would have ever caught his attention. Highlighting this same truth, John Tauler, a fourteenth-century Dominican monk, writes:

> God is a thousand times more intent upon making a man the masterpiece of His Divine art; and He does this by His strokes of suffering and His colors of pain. . . . Often human beings cannot tell whether they are seeking God's will or their own. Grievous suffering reveals the hand of God.[7]

Again, grievous suffering — even the suffering which grows out of ambition and envy — can bring great good. Though by itself it cannot solve the problem of evil, at least it can crack open the door of the kingdom of self.

THE GROUP DIMENSION

If individuals pursue their self-interest with unending energy, at times neglecting or perhaps violating the basic rights of others, social groups from ethnic subcultures up to nation states are even more prone to these tendencies. In other words, the forces of self-curvature, and therefore the potential for conflict, increase not arithmetically but geometrically as we move from the individual to the social group. Reinhold Niebuhr, perhaps America's greatest theologian, illustrates this dynamic in his important book *Moral Man and Immoral Society* written in 1932. Commenting on his fellow ethicists, both religious and secular, Niebuhr writes:

> What is lacking among all these moralists, whether religious or rational, is an understanding of the brutal character of the behavior of all human collectives, and the power of self-interest and collective egoism in all intergroup relations. Failure to recognize the stubborn resistance of group egoism to all moral and inclusive social objectives inevitably involves them in unrealistic and confused political thought.[8]

Furthermore, Niebuhr contends that his own age failed to realize that as individuals men and women at least believe that they ought to aim at love and justice and serve each other, even if their efforts are flagging. However, as racial, economic, and national groups, "they take for themselves, whatever their power can command."[9] Accordingly, diverse social groups will more likely than not pursue their own self-interest even at the expense of the good of the whole, what Rousseau called the common good. Unfortunately, this division of the social order into self-interested groups can breed an "us versus them" mentality which often increases resentment, strife, and alienation. Indeed, Arthur Schlesinger, Jr., an American historian, writes about the tribalization of American life currently underway in his book *The Disuniting of America.* Among other things, this celebrated scholar warns us that an undue emphasis on pluralism and diversity (e.g., racial, ethnic) may in the end undermine the bonds of social and political cohesion which hold us together. If we constantly emphasize our differences, the things that divide us, we may never achieve greater social harmony. The task then, according to Schlesinger, is to combine a healthy appreciation of the great diversity of the American nation with "due emphasis on the great unifying Western ideas of individual freedom, political democracy and human rights."[10]

Beyond this, one of the dynamics seldom noticed by commentators is that social groups, whether ethnic, racial, religious, or ideological, are often adept at masking their own will to power behind appeals to social justice, religion, or even reason. In fact, some activists will blatantly encourage many of these groups and subcultures, call for their "empowerment," and maintain that they are actually entitled to a larger share of the goods of society than others. And if other groups suffer at their expense, so be it. If different segments of the society are now denied equal access to public institutions and employment, it's a small price to be paid — or so we are told. However, it appears to be both irrational and immoral to maintain that one can eliminate prejudice against certain social groups by being prejudiced against others. Ethno-centrism is as equally deplorable as egotism; tribalism as equally despicable as selfishness. What is evil at the individual level can-not be good at the group level.

Observe, however, that these preceding observations are not meant to deny the very real and serious injustices that have been committed against certain social and ethnic groups in the past. However, a critical spirituality, in its attentiveness to the evil of the human heart and to the ethnocentrism (group self-interest) of social groups seeks to unmask self-absorption in any form or beneath any argument. It cannot be deterred from its probing examination by moral intimidation nor by specious, self-interest-ed argument. Where there is prejudice in any form, spirituality will renounce it regardless of the justification. Where there is injustice, it will correct it, but not by creating further injustice. And where there is advancement at the expense of the good of the whole, it will abhor it. In this respect, then, spirituality, as noted in passing in chapter 2, looks very much like the critical thinking movement which has received much of its energy from Richard Paul. On the nature of prejudice, Paul perceptively writes:

> *Blind* loyalty to a group is not, for example, a rational preference. Neither is the practice of giving preferred status in a society to particular ethnic and religious groups. A prejudiced preference, on the other hand, implies a preference based not on good reasons, but on considerations that will not stand up to critical assessment. We can not work against prejudice if we encourage the very pro-cesses that create it.[11]

In a real sense, then, the stance which a critical spirituality calls for in terms of larger social and political problems is a dynamic one. It offers neither a simplistic answer to social problems, nor does it have any favored groups. Rather, spirituality issues in a dialectic of yes/no to *all* groups seeking social benefits. Thus, where there has been or continues to be prejudice or discrimination against any people, spirituality supports them in their efforts for recourse and justice. However, spirituality also issues a negative word to these very same groups when they ignore the larger good of the whole and when they seek empowerment at the expense of others.

As men and women become more keenly aware of their own evil, as they discern the self-interested arguments of social and political groups, they will perhaps more zealously seek to remain real monotheists by locating God, the One who surpasses the divisions of group life and is, therefore, the basis for harmony, as the chief value around which all other values revolve. Race, gender, economic status, or any other penultimate element which is placed at the center is, therefore, deemed idolatrous. By any other name, self-centeredness remains self-centeredness. We need not find the very substance of our identity in group commitments.

SUMMING UP

In this chapter we have considered the various strategies which the self develops in order to deal with the insecurity of life, namely, by (a) claiming life is absurd, (b) pretending that the self is not limited, and (c) asserting the self ever more forcefully. Of these strategies, we have paid particular attention to the last one and demonstrated both on an individual and group level the discord in the form of envy, strife, and anger which are often left in the wake of selfish ambition.

In the next chapter, we will begin to examine the "awakened self," the one who realizes — often through suffering, failure and defeat — that his or her life is not as it should be. In particular, we will explore the initial — and vain — attempts of the self to heal itself by moralism, the practice of virtue, and by rigid adherence to orthodoxy. Beyond this, we will examine the conditions of presumption and despair which often emerge after the initial, self-led strategies collapse.

INDIVIDUAL OR GROUP REFLECTION QUESTIONS

1 Explore the ways in which we can hide our selfish ambition from ourselves and others. How do our families, schools, employment, and political institutions, at times, foster this spirit? Are children ever taught to excel in order to be loved? How is sinful ambition eventually exposed for what it is?

2 W.E. Sangster once wrote that "[jealousy] is a vice which takes no pleasure in itself. A proud man can enjoy his pride and a covetous man delight in his hoardings, but a jealous man gets nothing out of jealousy."[12] What do you think he meant?

3 When competitive people enter a social situation they can have the effect similar to a very large planet that draws everything into its orbit. Why are other people so easily drawn into this competitive spirit? What does this, perhaps, indicate about their self-understanding and their relation to God?

4 In Paul's letters to the Corinthians, it is evident that this early church was overrun with sinful strife and dissension. What was it that led to the disruption of fellowship in the Corinthian church? What did Paul advise in light of it? Can the lessons from this early church be applied to the church today? If so, how so? If not, why not?

5 Suggest ways in which groups can seek social justice without becoming self-absorbed or ethnocentric. How can an "us versus them" mentality be eliminated with respect to race, ethnicity, and gender by groups seeking the redress of their grievances?

FIVE

THE DELUSIONS OF THE SELF:
False Hope and Bad Faith

There is a way which seems right to a man, but in the end it leads to death" (Prov. 14:12).

The opening paragraph of John Calvin's memorable work, *Institutes of the Christian Religion,* expresses clearly and succinctly the nature of wisdom, and it consists of two parts: "the knowledge of God and of ourselves."[1] But just how do we acquire real self-knowledge, let alone knowledge of God, as long as we are under the addictive influence of sex, money, pleasure, and the pursuit of power? And how can we ever know the Almighty in a profound and meaningful way if we are caught up in the kingdom of self?

Fortunately, the illusions of the self-centered life can be exposed in three key ways. First of all, a life focused on pleasure, even in its more noble forms, can get a clue that something is fundamentally wrong by means of the experience of boredom. To use the terminology we introduced in chapter 3, the "aesthetic stage" of moral and spiritual development delights in the new, the exciting; it tries to keep life "pumped up," so to speak. But not all moments are either exciting or pleasurable. Life is not like that. Boredom, though it is an important clue, is first experienced as a threat, an enemy, something to be gotten rid of as soon as possible. When boredom, however, is allowed to do its illuminating work, it can actually disclose not only that the happiness of the self has been placed on the shaky and changing foundation of external conditions, but, more importantly, that a life so lived is actually in despair. The self has been sold off to the nearest pleasure, the latest excitement, or worse yet, to the applause of the crowd.

Second, as the last chapter briefly noted, the experience of anguish, the emotional trauma that comes from a significant loss, the pain which is born of strife and competitiveness, as well as the suffering which results from various addictions can all result in significant self-knowledge. Take the case of Julius for example. When I was serving as a college chaplain in North Carolina a few years ago, Julius came to me and began to relate a history of abuse that he had suffered as a child, his generally low self-esteem as a result of this, and his present problem with alcohol. Though all of his problems were significant, I was especially concerned with his drinking because when Julius drank, usually two or three times a week, he polished off a fifth of whiskey at a time. After much discussion and prayer, I gave Julius information about both professional and nonprofessional services in the area and urged him to seek counseling. But Julius continued to drink. And a pattern quickly emerged: Julius would get drunk, and when he had done things the night before that especially pained his conscience, he would wake up remorseful and call me on the phone. On one level, Julius knew that he was an alcoholic and that drinking was ruining his life, but on another level he liked alcohol so much that he was not about to stop. And it was not until he experienced the humiliation of being arrested for driving under the influence, the financial setback of increased insurance rates, and the general disgust of those he loved, that Julius finally entered a treatment program. Suffering had done its work well; the message got through. It showed one man, at least, the lie of the life he had been living—but would it be enough? Conviction of evil does not always translate into lifelong reform.

Third, since the aesthetic stage values openness, freedom, possibility, lack of commitment, and keeping reality (especially death) at a distance, there is a sense in which this stage is typical of youth (although the aesthetic stage can characterize any age).[2]

Indeed, it appears that the aging process itself, if taken seriously, can clear away many of the illusions of youth and help us to see life much more clearly and realistically. Time can teach us many things if we are willing to listen. A young man, for example, may move from relationship to relationship in a lighthearted way, but the married man in choosing one woman has denied all others. He has made a fruitful but binding commitment. Again, a young woman may fantasize about being a doctor, a biologist, or an engineer, but the older woman has already made her decision about career and is living with the consequences. Her options are much less open; her horizon less broad; she knows the reality of decision and responsibility.

Moreover, for many people, with age comes a greater awareness of their own mortality, a greater sense that time is running out. For instance, when we were younger, we often thought we were immortal, and time seemed to go by ever so slowly. Summer vacation was an eternity, and fifth grade seemed like a decade. But now that we are older, the aches and pains in our body, that washed-out feeling that comes and goes, and our slower recovery from hard physical exercise lets us know that youth is slipping away. Time moves us along, and we now have a greater understanding where it is leading us.

In order, then, to grow older with a sense of integrity we must learn to *accept* the greater burdens, responsibilities, as well as the limited options, the decrease in vigor and physical attractiveness that all come with age. And for those who in young adulthood or later are willing to throw off many of the illusions of youth (immortality being the chief one) and who are also willing to accept the limitations of decision and commitment, they will begin to realize that life is much more serious than they thought at first. This coupled with an increased sense of their own mortality, opens them up to what Sören Kierkegaard called the "ethical stage" of moral and spiritual development. Here people see more clearly the significance of values and the worth of principles. They begin to cherish universal ideals and to delight in virtue. On the other hand, they keenly sense the guilt which continues to plague their consciences and the shame which they feel before others for failure to realize those very same ideals.

Although he used slightly different terminology from that of Kierkegaard, John Wesley, the father of Methodism, portrayed the same dynamics of this process quite accurately. In his sermon, "The Spirit of Bondage and of Adoption," Wesley marks the transition from the natural state (roughly equivalent to Kierkegaard's aesthetic stage) to the legal state (Kierkegaard's ethical stage) in the following words.

> Here ends his pleasing dream, his delusive rest, his false peace, his vain security. His joy now vanishes as a cloud; pleasures once loved delight no more. . . . The fumes of those opiates being now dispelled, he feels the anguish of a wounded spirit. He finds that sin let loose upon the soul (whether it be pride, anger, or evil desire; whether self-will, malice, envy, revenge, or any other) is perfect misery. He feels sorrow of heart . . . remorse . . . fear. . . .[3]

Yet another characteristic of the ethical or conventional stage is the attempt to bring reality in relation to the ideal. Put another way, it is the attempt to have our actions match the high principles which we now hold. In this sense, the ethical stage seeks virtue, and it often follows the pattern of what is good and respectable in society. It is the cry of the drug addict who wants to reform; the pain and loneliness of the proud who seeks relief; and the plea of the self-serving for liberation from this awful captivity. And though there are problems even with this stage of development, as will be apparent shortly, it is the only basis upon which society is possible. Men and women must aim at virtue, but they must aim at something higher as well.

So then, the experience of boredom, suffering, and anguish, as well as the prospect of growing older, can at times precipitate an awakening, a crisis, in men and women such that they are now willing to grow along spiritual lines or at least along ethical ones. The church calls such willingness to change and grow "repentance," a turning away from sin and toward God, and it is the passageway to all spiritual life. Truth be told, none are excepted from its necessity, and there can be little advance in grace without it.

DETOURS ALONG THE WAY

As important a step as an awakening to spiritual reality is, it is no guarantee that the potent evil described in this book will then lose its hold. Sorrow for sin, remorse for past failures, and firm resolutions ("I will stop, I promise") will not by themselves heal the deep and critical problem of the soul. Something else is required beyond the self-knowledge which arises out of guilt and shame. However, this "something else" has been almost studiously neglected by some secular and religious counselors in their confrontation with human evil.

During the 1970s, for instance, the "non-directive," or "client-centered" approach of Carl Rogers was perhaps at the peak of its influence. And for those who continue to use this method, therapists are never so forward as to give actual advice or counsel to patients. Instead, they act much like a mirror reflecting the patients back to themselves in order that they may come to greater insight and self-awareness. In this context, then, the personal autonomy (independence) of men and women is both respected and affirmed. Rogers explains:

> If I can create a relationship characterized on my part by a genuineness and transparency, in which I am my real feelings; by a warm acceptance of and prizing of the other person as a separate individual; by a sensitive ability to see his world and himself as he sees them; then the other individual in the relationship: will experience and understand aspects of himself which previously he has repressed; will find himself becoming better integrated, more able to function effectively; will become more similar to the person he would like to be; will be more self-directing and self-confident; will become more of a person, more unique and more self-expressive; will be more understanding, more acceptant of others; [and] will be able to cope with the problems of life more adequately and more comfortably.[4]

Observe, however, the excessive claims which are made on behalf of the patient in light of a change in behavior on the part of the *counselor*. Oddly enough, it is the *patient* who is now better integrated, able to function more effectively, and who is more self-confident. But the attempt to cure significant evil, whether it be in the form of enslaving lust or hateful pride, by some form of "insight therapy" where the troubled soul is merely equipped with greater *knowledge* of its predicament will not, by itself, undo the shackles of even some of the more common forms of evil. There are all too many men and women today who know quite clearly that they are in the grip of evil—and even how and why they got there—and yet they can find no release. Commenting on a similar dynamic in the first century the Apostle Paul writes:

> We know that the law is spiritual; but I am unspiritual, sold as a slave to sin. I do not understand what I do. For what I want to do I do not do, but what I hate I do. And if I do what I do not want to do, I agree that the law is good. As it is, it is no longer I myself who do it, but it is sin living in me. I know that nothing good lives in me, that is, in my sinful nature. *For I have the desire to do what is good, but I cannot carry it out.* For what I do is not the good I want to do; no, the evil I do not want to do—this I keep on doing (Rom. 7:14-19).[5]

The problem of the soul, in other words, is not at its essence a lack of knowledge—though knowledge is, after all, important and helpful—but the human will which has been corrupted and enslaved. But just how does one change the will, especially when it is divided, that is, when one part of the will wants to reform, but another part doesn't? Put another way, how does one *will* to change one's will? This question must eventually be addressed by every form of counseling, both secular and religious.

In the three "detours" which follow, we will describe a few of the more common ways in which people who are earnestly seeking spiritual, emotional, and psychological wholeness can become sidetracked with the unfortunate result that the evil in their lives, despite their best intentions, will continue virtually unchecked. This problem is further complicated once it is realized that each of the three detours below is an important emphasis in its own right. Difficulty occurs, however, when each of these emphases offers itself as *the* solution to human evil.

Moralism

During the Enlightenment of the eighteenth century, Immanuel Kant called for humanity's release from a self-imposed slavery, that is, from "man's inability to make use of his understanding without direction from another."[6] "*Sapere Aude!*" or "dare to reason" was the rallying cry of the age. However, in this clarion call for change there was not only an emphasis on human independence which emerged out of the self-sufficiency of reason, but also a discounting of the transcendent or the supernatural. Humanity, not God, was to be the principal agent here, and appeals to the Holy Spirit were quietly put aside. "Thinking for one's self," Kant writes, "means to seek the supreme touchstone of truth in one's self; i.e. in one's own reason — and the following of the maxim of always thinking for one's self is enlightenment. . . ."[7] Accordingly, for this eighteenth-century philosopher men and women are not so much in a dependent relation to a Holy God through faith as they are in relation to a moral order which they can know through the use of their own reason.

Moreover, for Kant, as with many other thinkers of this period, since people can know the moral order, they are in turn obligated to fulfill its demands. Here the emphasis is on commitment and duty. The "horizontal" dimension of human relations has apparently edged out "the vertical" dimension of the power and favor of God; self-effort has replaced divine grace. Consequently, in his book *Religion within the Limits of Reason Alone* Kant writes: "True religion is to consist not in the knowing or considering what God does or has done for our salvation, but in what we must do to become worthy of it."[8] Religion's role, then, is a largely subservient one: it is to inculcate and support ethics. It does not lead to anything (or anyone) higher than human effort.

Though the interrelation between religion and ethics is by no means denied, there is a sense in which religion, in the best sense of the word, goes far beyond ethics in its emphasis on spirituality and devotion to God. That is, though one can be an ethical person without religion (many atheists, for example, are very moral people who live according to the rule to bring about the greatest good for the greatest number of people), one cannot grow spiritually simply by focusing on ethics. Transcendence —

that is, getting beyond and outside oneself through the worship of God—is also necessary. This indeed is part of the contribution that religion can make to the well-rounded life that cannot be made by ethics alone.

Ultimately, Kant's thought has not only had a significant impact on those thinkers who looked with disfavor on the Middle Ages, especially in terms of its spirituality and supposed superstition, but also on many leaders in the modern church. Thus, Ritschl, Harnack, and other theologians of the nineteenth and twentieth centuries have all been influenced by Kant's judgment on the relation of religion to ethics. More to the point, when this influence is translated into contemporary pulpits it usually takes the form of some sort of moralism or admonition to virtue: live a good life, be a good citizen, help your neighbor, give to a charity. And though this preaching is very clear on what we should do, and this is truly praiseworthy, it is less clear in terms of how we shall ever bring it about. Thus, if the Christian religion is reduced by being made subservient to ethics, if Christ merely becomes, in the words of Rousseau, "the teacher and pattern of pure and lofty morality,"[9] a mere prophet, then men and women will inevitably be thrown back on their own resources as they struggle to imitate Christ and to fulfill His high moral demands. But will the efforts of those who have encountered radical evil ever be enough to liberate them? Saint Cyprian said it well, "No one is safe by his own strength, but he is safe by the grace and mercy of God." The following chart illustrates the difference between religion which places a premium on ethics and self-effort and religion which highlights spirituality and transcendence.

Ethical Religion	*Spiritual Religion*
The self is at center	God is at center
The "I" is the doer of the good	God is the doer of the good
The self is related to a set of principles or rules	The self is related to a God
Stresses virtue	Stresses faith
Opposite of sin is virtue	Opposite of sin is faith
Content with conventional morality	Not content with conventional morality

Moralism, then, whether in a secular or religious form, virtually leaves the kingdom of self intact as it directs the self to realize the good by using its *own* reason and abilities. A relationship to laws, principles, and abstractions has been substituted for a relationship to Christ. The divine/human relation, in other words, has been replaced by a human/legal one. Thus, if there is any advance toward the good, it must be accomplished by the "I" which has been left very much at the center of things. This characteristic, coupled with an enduring optimism about the goodness of human nature, makes all moralism, whether on the personal or social level, look naive. But what if the problem is actually within oneself, with a divided and corrupted will as suggested earlier? How, then, will people ever realize the ethical ideal? Part of the self wants to achieve the ideal; the other part wants to be free of it. In short, moralism, reliance on human ability, repeatedly underestimates both the potency and resiliency of evil in human lives. It relies on self-effort where self-effort will no longer work. And in the end it will leave the addict with his needles and the prostitute in her bed.

Orthodoxy
A second way in which those who are eager to reform their lives are led astray in frustration and disappointment is through the glorification of orthodoxy. In some fundamentalist churches today, for example, great stress is laid on the correctness of belief where all the "i's" are dotted and all the "t's" are crossed. That is, one must believe the right "things" in order to be redeemed. In a way reminiscent of Protestant scholasticism of the late sixteenth century, belief becomes, to a significant degree, a matter of assenting to propositions or statements that have been carefully crafted—and some not so carefully crafted—by the church leadership.

The great danger in this position is that an undue emphasis on correctness of belief can easily become confused with redemption itself. Though perhaps unintended, salvation will soon be identified, at least in the minds of some, with affirming proper doctrines, with assenting to articles of faith. Consequently, one will know that one is a Christian precisely because one believes such and such. But will a "gospel" so conceived liberate? Will rational assent to truth break the power of evil? Let me tell you a story.

A few years back I was a part of a Bible study group which met once a week at an artist's house in Brooklyn, New York. At this study I encountered a young man named Tom who was inquisitive, troubled, and "giving Christianity one last shot" as he put it. At first, Tom would not tell me what he had meant by that last comment, except that he was very disappointed with the churches he had been attending. In time, however, as I gained his confidence, Tom opened up.

One of the things which destroyed Tom's serenity and which made him feel guilty and alienated from God was his problem with impure thoughts and the masturbation which often followed them. Oddly enough, one pastor of a large mainline denomination told him that masturbation was normal, a part of growing up, and that he would soon get over it. But Tom knew that his masturbation was not normal, and it was beginning to get out of control. And besides, this young man of sixteen did not at all appreciate the pastor's attempt to make light of what was for him a very serious matter.

A few months after this incident, Tom started attending a fundamentalist, congregational church. Soon he cut his hair, began to dress differently, stopped attending movies, passed out tracts, but he continued to masturbate—though not as frequently. When he finally worked up the courage, Tom spoke to his new minister about his problem. Unlike the previous pastor, this fundamentalist pastor took Tom seriously. In fact, he told him, in more or less words, that what Tom was doing was sinful and that if he didn't stop he would go to hell.

With redoubled effort, Tom became obsessed with stopping; he tried to reform, but couldn't. He promised himself he would remain pure. He even vowed to God one night that he would never engage in this practice again, but his resolutions quickly evaporated in the face of powerful and consuming desires. He was especially perplexed because he was trying so hard and yet he seemed to get nowhere. He was a member of a local church, he believed that Jesus Christ is the Son of God, he affirmed the Resurrection, the Virgin Birth, and the second coming of Christ;

he believed it was sinful for men to wear their hair long, and he assented to many of the other fundamentalist taboos, but still he found no relief. The more he struggled against sin, the more did he feel its chains. But no one could tell this young man that he wasn't earnest or sincere.

To be sure, Tom's problem was that he lacked power—a power which he later received as he made the chief object of his faith and trust not doctrines, but *the person* of Jesus Christ. But this took time—a lot of time. Commenting on a similar problem in his own day, John Wesley cautioned against making a religion out of correct belief, a practice which, no doubt, affects the mind, but which leaves the heart and will virtually untouched. In his sermon "On the Wedding Garment," written in 1790, Wesley explains:

> When things of an *indifferent nature* are represented as necessary to salvation it is a folly of the same kind, though not of the same magnitude. . . . Among these we may undoubtedly rank *orthodoxy*, or right opinions. We know indeed that wrong opinions in religion naturally lead to wrong tempers, or wrong practices; and that consequently it is our bounden duty to pray that we may have a right judgment in all things. But still a man may judge as accurately as the devil, and yet be as wicked as he.[10]

Again in another sermon, "The Way to the Kingdom," Wesley points out that the nature of true religion lies not in correct opinions, however noble they may be, but in the human heart.

> So manifest it is that although true religion naturally leads to every good word and work, yet the real nature thereof lies deeper still, even in "the hidden man of the heart."
>
> I say of the *heart*. For neither does religion consist in *orthodoxy* or *right opinions* . . . He may assent to all the three creeds—that called the Apostles', the Nicene, and the Athanasian—and yet 'tis possible he may have no religion at all. . . .[11]

Lest there be misunderstanding, it must be noted that Wesley is not suggesting that doctrinal belief is unimportant—nor am I.

In fact, he later writes that theological indifference and unsettledness is a great curse and not a blessing. The Apostles' Creed—like other expressions of faith—is, after all, significant. What he is suggesting, however, is that faith must not only involve the mind, but it must engage the heart as well; it must touch the deepest recesses of our being and character. In a similar fashion, the letter of James reminds us: "You believe that there is one God. Good! Even the demons believe *that*—and shudder" (James 2:19).[12] The Gospel, then, is not an opinion we hold, a speculative thing, a matter of debating points. It is nothing less than the grace of God manifested in the person of Jesus Christ, by whom the captives can be set free. The Gospel orients us not so much to an object as to a person. The Gospel, then, is not so much belief *that* as it is belief *in*. And this is the crucial lesson which Tom eventually learned.

Sacramentalism

A third way in which those who are eager to reform their lives can be misdirected from the heart of the Gospel and eventually frustrated is through sacramentalism. However, in order to be clear at this point, a distinction must be made between the sacraments as a vital means of grace and sacramentalism which is quite a different thing and whose major focus, despite protests to the contrary, is not the divine/human relationship—characterized by grace, personal faith, and trust—but the proper performance of an institutional ritual.

On the one hand, the sacraments of baptism and the Lord's Supper are a necessary means in the Christian life which can convey nothing less than the rich grace of God to us. Indeed, the sacraments, so understood, are the conduits, the chief vehicles, through which the bounty, favor, and power of God are communicated. Therefore, all those who minimize the necessity of these means of grace do so at their own peril. Without the sacraments as a means of grace, we run the risk of isolation from the community of faith and we, therefore, court the prospect of fanaticism.

In sacramentalism, on the other hand, far more concern is expressed over the proper form of the ritual, who performs it, and what "objectively" takes place by means of its performance.

The danger here, of course, is one of formalism. That is, the sacrament can begin to be viewed as an end in itself rather than as a means, with the result that it will soon lose its connection to the God/human *relationship*. A clear expression of this tendency can be found in the medieval practice of the private mass, a ritual which the priest performed utterly alone, apart from the community of faith. The sacrament, at least in this instance, had truly taken on a life of its own. Not surprisingly, this aberrant practice, which forgot that communion always necessitates a living community with Christ as its head, was rightly rejected by Martin Luther and other reformers of the church.

On the contemporary scene, the issue of sacramentalism comes into sharpest focus, perhaps, in the ongoing practice of infant baptism and in the consequences for our understanding of redemption which flow from it. The Roman Catholic tradition, for instance, clearly teaches baptismal regeneration. In other words, when an infant is baptized, it is at that time born of God. Again, according to Catholic doctrine, "Baptism is the sacrament of spiritual regeneration by which a person is incorporated in Christ and made a member of his Mystical Body, given grace, and cleared of original sin."[13]

In a similar fashion, *The Book of Discipline* of the United Methodist Church states that "the pastor of each charge shall earnestly exhort all Christian parents or guardians to present their children to the Lord in Baptism at *an early age*."[14] That infant baptism is actually a sacrament by proxy, a remnant of the old Constantinian state church (and earlier) which has been mediated to Methodism through its Anglican heritage, is revealed by the *Discipline's* further instructions, namely, that "the pastor shall diligently instruct the parents or guardians regarding the meaning of this Sacrament and the vows which *they* assume."[15]

Presently, the United Methodist Church is in the midst of heated controversy about a proper understanding of baptism, and a study commission has been appointed to explore the issue. Some leaders in the denomination, for instance, argue for infant baptismal regeneration—much like Roman Catholicism—and they, therefore, want the *Discipline* to be more specific in this regard. Still others, like those who have recently signed *The*

Memphis Declaration, maintain that "baptism is a means of God's grace, but that a personal decision to accept Jesus Christ as Savior and Lord is essential for salvation and for full membership in the Church." And so the debate continues.

Though this clearly is not the place to entertain a full discussion, one way or the other, on the merits of infant baptism, nevertheless, a few points need to be made as they pertain to our larger topic. First of all, one of the dangers of sacramentalism, and of the practice of infant baptism in particular, is that the church may end up with a very impersonal understanding of redemption, one that neglects the crucial roles of the grace of God and personal faith. That is, it may suggest unwittingly that one is redeemed precisely *because* one has been baptized or *because* one continues to receive the Lord's Supper. Here we come very close to an *ex opere operato* view of the sacraments, that grace is conferred and received merely by the performance of the ritual. Equally troubling, we may intimate or suggest that salvation, freedom from the guilt and power of sin, is guaranteed by good churchmanship. However, how many have knelt at the altar rail only to get up from it unreformed?

A second danger in sacramentalism is that the impersonal flavor, the diminishment of personal faith which often marks infant baptism, can be carried over to views of adult baptism as well — with disastrous consequences for the body of Christ. To illustrate this last point, let me again tell you a story. When a man whom I loved and respected died after a long illness of much suffering and distress, a wake was held and a priest was invited to speak to the mourners as is the custom among Irish Catholics. The priest, a middle-aged and sincere man, told us that Gerard — no one ever called this man by that name — was an heir of eternal life because he had "been baptized into Christ's church" and "had eaten the sacred body of our Redeemer." Never once did the priest talk of the life or faith of this man. Never once did he mention this man's struggle with death and the grace of God he had received through this struggle. But how would the priest have spoken if his understanding of salvation was informed not so much by the normative status of infant baptism, but by something so challenging as adult baptism where baptismal grace is never separated from the faith that receives it? To be sure, faith does not make the sacrament, but faith receives the sacrament. One does not have to be a Baptist to appreciate the vital issues here.

Furthermore, Emil Brunner continually cautioned his readers—and his congregation in Zurich—about the impersonality which sets in as a result of institutionalism. Indeed, it is no mistake that the most institutional and established churches are also some of the strongest defenders of infant baptism. But as Brunner reminds us, "Above all it is impossible to harmonize Paul's teaching about faith and in particular his explicit teaching about Baptism with the thought of Infant Baptism."[16] And in response to his critics who saw a model for infant baptism in the Old Testament practice of circumcision, Brunner writes:

> For this is the new thing in the Ekklesia (the Church) in contrast with Israel, that one does not enter the people of God by being born but by being born again, i.e. through faith. The sign of circumcision has nothing to do with faith; it was applied, so to speak, *ex opere operato.* Also the thought that the fellowship or the "house" believes for the infant did indeed correspond to a concept of solidarity like that of the Old Testament, but not to Paul's concept of faith which equates being baptized with dying with Christ.[17]

In fact, in his book *The Divine-Human Encounter,* Brunner, not a man known for intemperate speech, concluded that "the contemporary practice of infant baptism can hardly be regarded as being anything short of scandalous."[18]

Third, to insinuate to people who are in the grip of potent evil that they are *already* redeemed and born of God or to imply that they are presently righteous, having been baptized as infants, is to undermine their hope for future liberation from sin and evil. Even John Wesley, the high churchman that he was, understood this dynamic well and wrote in his sermon, "The Marks of the New Birth" the following admonition.

> Say not then in your heart, I *was once* baptized; therefore I am now a child of God. Alas, that consequence will by no means hold.

How many are the baptized gluttons and drunkards, the baptized
liars and common swearers, the baptized railers and evil-speakers,
the baptized whoremongers, thieves, extortioners! What think
you? Are these now the children of God?[19]

The best indicator, perhaps, that one belongs to Christ and is a
part of His body, the church, is not the reception of baptism nor
even participating in the Lord's Supper — though these sacraments are clearly valuable — but union with Christ through a faith
which is active in love. The sacraments, in other words, are a
significant *means* of grace, and they should be celebrated and
used as such by all earnest believers who seek to grow in the
image and likeness of God. Nevertheless, if the sacraments are
treated as the end or goal of faith, instead of as a *means* of grace,
all sorts of distortions in the life of the church will occur. The
chief object of the sinner's heart, then, that to which it should be
continually directed, is not to a ritual or a means of grace, but to
the end or goal of that ritual, the person of Jesus Christ.

GIVING UP ON GRACE:
SLOTH, PRESUMPTION, AND DESPAIR

When religion is understood chiefly in terms of moralism, rigid
orthodoxy, and sacramentalism, this understanding constitutes
the insidious error of formalism. Sadly I have encountered all too
many people in my own counseling experience who have suffered
under this misdirection. Here men and women have the appropriate *form* of religion, but they lack its suitable *power*. Indeed,
though these unfortunate people have all the formal trappings of
religion, they are nevertheless without the vitality which scriptural Christianity should always instill. And continuing down this
same course for months or perhaps even years will only have a
deadening effect: it will sap all the energy for reform which was
present at the outset. Indeed, in time a kind of spiritual sloth, a
laziness, will set in as these outwardly religious people fail to
undertake a spiritual quest to develop their interior life and as
they, on the other hand, begin to hide behind the external elements of religion in order to avoid facing their true spiritual

condition. Here, odd as it may seem, religion itself will become a mask, a facade, under which lies the continuing presence of sin and evil.

There are two key dangers which can result from this spiritual laziness, this abandonment of the ongoing task of reform, this stubborn desire to remain on the ethical or conventional level. First of all, when the essence of religion is equated with formalism, the specter of *presumption* (assuming we are righteous in the sight of God when we are not) is never far behind. But before this deadly sin can take root, the outwardly religious person must first of all compartmentalize the evil which remains in his or her life and then identify with "the good side." Once this is done, outward appearances can be maintained, and the soul can then be left to indulge its secret sins with little anxiety or trouble to the conscience. Beyond this, the illusion of righteousness can be held in place, at least for a time, by comparing oneself with other people: "I'm not as bad as so and so"; by lowering the scriptural standards of Christianity: "I'm only human"; or by taking offense at the Gospel when it is presented in its fullness and holiness.

Though it is similar to presumption in equating the heart of religion with formalism, despair, the second danger of spiritual sloth, breaks through the dull and sleepy world of presumption and recognizes on some level that evil has not been overcome, that it remains a potent, destructive, and (from its perspective) unconquerable force in human life. Again, unlike presumption, spiritual despair breaks through the facade of righteousness, comprehends the nature and extent of ongoing evil, but then erroneously concludes that since religion "has been tried" there is little or no hope. Guilt, undoubtedly, looms large here since the moral and spiritual ideals of the self have not been achieved. Indeed, failing to take into account, in a significant way, what good does remain, the despairing self — oddly enough — has now become its own judge and executioner. Pierre Charron described this dynamic in his writings quite well: "Despair is like forward children, who, when you take away one of their playthings, throw the rest into the fire for madness. It grows angry with itself, turns its own executioner, and revenges its misfortunes on its own head." In other words, unable to achieve an ideal good, the self forsakes the hope of any good. Nevertheless, despair with its painful guilt may ironically lead one toward the kingdom of God. It perhaps can realize, in a way in which the presumptive self cannot, the bankruptcy of the kingdom of self, the futility of all schemes of self-redemption. It then may be open to the prospect of faith in and surrender to a holy God.

So then, in the face of such spiritual sloth, presumption, and despair what is needed is not more formalism, not more empty religiosity, not more external religion, but nothing less than inward, spiritual religion. This must be a religion which will motivate us to face honestly the evil in our lives, but which will then offer hope; it must be a religion which will direct us to the love of neighbor and to a holy God as the One who can deliver us from evil, and, finally, it must be a religion which will undermine all forms of complacency and self-satisfaction by ever challenging us to move forward in our spiritual journey. What is needed, in other words, is a religion which will not be ashamed of developing the interior life, of fostering holy tempers in the human heart, and of responding to God's grace through faith. But is the contemporary Western church poised to meet this need? Does it even understand the problem?

SPIRITUALITY AND THE FUTURE OF MAINLINE DENOMINATIONS

Social scientists and pollsters tell us that if present trends continue the composition of the American church will be much different in the twenty-first century. Mainline denominations like the United Methodist Church, the Presbyterian Church in the United States of America, the Episcopal Church, and the recently reconstituted Lutheran churches are all in serious decline. To illustrate, George Gallup points out in a recent survey of American religion that "the most dramatic findings were that one in three Americans who were raised Methodist and one in ten who were raised Catholic no longer identify with those churches."[20] At the same time, conservative and evangelical bodies, like the Church of the Nazarene, which have placed a premium on spirituality, are prospering. In their best-selling book *Megatrends 2000,* Naisbitt and Aburdene note these shifts as well and write:

> Evangelical churches have gained 10 million people in the past ten
> years. Every five years since 1965 the evangelicals have grown 8
> percent, while mainline Protestants have lost 5 percent. There are
> 40 million evangelicals in the United States, according to the
> National Association of Evangelicals in Washington, D.C.[21]

In response to this decline, there has been a spate of books and
articles by denominational leaders which attempt to grapple with
this ongoing problem. For some, the solution is to play with the
institutional machinery: change a board here, add a new one
there, reshuffle a few offices, and the like. Others, like J. Edward
Carothers, maintain that mainstream churches are faltering because they have failed to "open up the hidden doubts of the laity
and clergy and . . . [they, therefore,] must find ways to encourage
the people to speak out in candor about their true beliefs and
fearful doubts"[22] — something like a John A.T. Robinson's *Honest
to God* come to Sunday School. Indeed, Carothers maintains that
it is important to encourage people to express their doubts about
"prayer, death, resurrection, heaven, hell, and all of the rest of
the very long list,"[23] as a cure for present ills.

However, in conducting workshops in local churches I find that
people's doubts are of a much different kind. They doubt that
ethics are relative, a matter of personal taste. They doubt that
this life is all there is, that death is *the* ultimate reality, a god, the
last word on things. They doubt the pronouncements of some
scientists which reject the reality of spirit and God. But most
importantly of all, perhaps, many of the men and women who sit
in the pews on Sunday mornings are beginning to doubt where
their present church leadership is taking them. They are, in
other words, doubting the doubters.

In fact, when a more professional and objective analysis of the
contemporary church situation is made which moves beyond the
confines of denominational self-analysis, we find a frank admis-
sion about the nature of the problem. George Gallup, for instance, observes in his book *The People's Religion* that "one of
the top three reasons why Americans leave the church is that
they want deeper spiritual meaning."[24] "Americans have become

more critical of their churches and synagogues over the past decade," he writes. "A large majority believes the churches are too concerned with internal organizational issues and not sufficiently concerned with spiritual matters."[25] In a similar fashion, Naisbitt and Aburdene point out that "college-educated people are particularly critical of [a] lack of spiritual nurturing,"[26] in the churches today. Moreover, these same authors conclude that many Americans are becoming dissatisfied with the traditional mainline churches for failing to explore "the link between their everyday lives and the transcendent."[27]

The problem in the American churches, then, really is one of confidence. But not in the way Carothers and others suspect. The common people are walking away from the up-to-date, politicized church because it neglects their deepest spiritual needs, ignores the transcendent, and elevates not divine power but human power. Human utopias, however, are no substitute for the kingdom of God. Consequently, deep in their hearts the common people realize, like their Christian brothers and sisters before them, that the weakness of God is far stronger than all human power, and that the foolishness of the Gospel is far more effective than the wisdom of this world. They want nothing less than real, vital, scriptural Christianity — without compromise, apology, or dilution. They are hungry, in other words, for spirituality — a kind of spirituality which will deliver and set the captives free. They need a spirituality that nurtures *soul care*.

SUMMING UP

In this chapter we have explored the various detours along the way as the self earnestly engages in particularly religious attempts at reform: moralism, orthodoxy, and sacramentalism. In addition, we have taken notice of some of the consequences of the self's efforts to heal itself, namely, spiritual sloth, presumption, and despair.

In the following chapter, then, we will begin to consider the principal solution to human evil, one which will lead us out of the kingdom of self to a much different destination — the kingdom of God. It is Jesus Christ who will point the way.

INDIVIDUAL OR GROUP REFLECTION QUESTIONS

1 If spirituality is defined, in a general fashion, as an awareness of God, self, and our neighbors that ever involves the element of transcendence, what then does it mean to transcend self and society? In what way is God transcendent? In addition, what are the practices which will help to foster such an awareness?

2 Sören Kierkegaard taught that the opposite of sin is not virtue, but faith. What are the implications of this judgment for conventional Christianity and for moralism? What is the difference between having virtue and having faith? How does virtue hide sin?

3 If the term "worldview" is defined as our most basic orientation to reality, consider the worldview offered in American culture (e.g., film, books, the media, higher education). Does this worldview acknowledge the reality of spirit? If so, indicate how so. If not, indicate why not. What are the implications of either judgment?

4 An increasing number of voices today contend that liberation theology has politicized the Gospel and that existential concerns like meaning, anxiety, fear of death, and guilt are being seriously neglected in this new orientation. What do you see as the implications of these trends?

5 What are some of the basic problems inherent in all self-help and self-reform strategies?

SIX

THE KINGDOM OF GOD:

The Cross of Christ and the Gift of Faith

For we know that our old self was crucified with him so that the body of sin might be done away with, that we should no longer be slaves to sin" (Rom. 6:6).

It should be evident by now that when we encounter significant evil in our lives, the way back to righteousness and peace is often strewn with numerous obstacles which prevent an easy solution to this problem. It seems, at times, as if we have entered a giant maze and we can no longer find the way out. Our good intentions vanish and our best resolve weakens under the enduring power of evil. Like Adam and Eve cast out of the Garden of Eden, we find the way to the tree of life barred by fiery angels. We genuinely desire life in its richness as it was meant to be lived, but we are unable to enjoy it.

If this were not enough, the human predicament is further complicated and worsened by the remembrance of past evil. Guilt, sorrow, and shame flood the soul eliminating any sense of well-being. Self-effort and moral reform have by now run their course with little effect, and they remain powerless to quiet the wrenching voices of lingering guilt. As St. Anselm, archbishop of Canterbury, realized centuries ago, even if men and women were from this point on to be utterly obedient to a holy God, this faithfulness would not itself make up for any past sin, and the guilt which inevitably follows, because all their obedience is owed to God anyway so that there is nothing "extra" to offer up. Indeed, the more we struggle against the chains of sin and guilt, the more do we feel them.

But there is hope. As Paul points out in 2 Corinthians, not all sorrow is detrimental. The apostle makes a distinction between "worldly sorrow" which leads to death and "godly sorrow," which leads to life and peace:

> Godly sorrow brings repentance that leads to salvation and leaves no regret, but worldly sorrow brings death. See what this godly sorrow has produced in you: what earnestness, what eagerness to clear yourselves, what indignation, what alarm, what longing, what concern, what readiness to see justice done (2 Cor. 7:8-11).

The Greek word used for repentance here is *metanoia* and it basically means "to have a change of heart or mind." In addition, *metanoia* can mean "to turn around," "to face a different direction," and it, therefore, marks the normal prelude to any significant appropriation of grace. In a real sense, this change in direction, of which Paul writes, involves facing *away* from self-effort and self-justification and facing *toward* the grace of God manifested in Jesus Christ. It is here that we begin to realize, in other words, that the way back to God, to life, and to wholeness is not direct, as we had once supposed, but indirect. Try as we may, we cannot do it by ourselves.

Why Is a Mediator Necessary?

The Bible reveals that human sin has caused an estrangement, an alienation between God and humanity. This divorce of the Most High and humanity, this breach of a proper relation, can be understood from two directions. From an "objective perspective," which is chiefly concerned with the offense committed against a transcendent God, the question becomes how will the divine righteousness and holiness be taken seriously in light of human evil and rebellion? From a "subjective perspective," on the other hand, the human side of the relation, the question becomes how can guilt be overcome so that men and women will not only trust in the God whom they have offended, but love Him as well?

The theologian who grappled with the first aspect of this dilemma, the objective elements, was St. Anselm of Canterbury. Maintaining that a reestablishment of the divine/human relation in righteousness is not an easy matter but quite difficult, St. Anselm wrote that "If anybody imagines that God can simply forgive us as we forgive others, that person has not yet considered the seriousness of sin."[1] Why is this so? In the first place, divine forgiveness cannot come as a matter of course simply because the offense which has been committed is so great: that is, humans, through their unbelief and willful rebellion, have not only cast aspersion on the goodness and holiness of their Creator, but they have also flouted the just and righteous moral order of the universe.

Second, divine forgiveness should not be equated with or reduced to the level of human forgiveness (the latter often being a form of indulgence or permissiveness) and then be expected as a matter of course simply because the goodness and holiness of God far surpass what we could ever imagine. To be sure, it is one thing to sin against a mortal creature; it is quite another thing, however, to sin against the eternal God, the infinite and beneficent Creator, the one who transcends us in glory, whose "eyes are too pure to look on evil" (Hab. 1:13). Cheap forgiveness, then, like the cheap grace upon which it is based, takes neither the righteousness nor the awe-inspiring holiness of God into account. It fails to consider, in other words, against *whom* we have sinned.

Third, that God takes His own justice and holiness seriously, even if men and women do not, is revealed in the numerous instances, not a few, in which Scripture explores the wrath of God Almighty. The *New International Version*, for example, uses the English word "wrath" over twenty-five times, a fact which, no doubt, proves troubling for those contemporary theologians who continue to deny, in the face of considerable evidence, this important aspect of the divine character. More to the point, in the New Testament, there are basically two Greek words which are behind the English translation of "wrath." The first word, *org,* is used over two dozen times, and it is most often translated as "wrath," although sometimes it is rendered by the English word "anger." The second Greek word, which is used much less often, is *thumos* and it too is translated as both "wrath" and "anger." And though these two Greek terms are, at times, translated by the same English word, the differences between them in meaning are important — differences which can help us to understand the wrath of God aright. W.E. Vine explains:

> *Thumos* . . . is to be distinguished from *org*, in this respect, that *thumos* indicates a more agitated condition of the feelings, an outburst of wrath from inward indignation, while *org* suggests a more settled or abiding condition of mind. . . . *Org* is less sudden in its rise than *thumos*, but more lasting in its nature.[2]

The significance of this distinction, then, is that the principal word which the New Testament uses to refer to the wrath of God, *org*, depicts not an agitated outburst, not a hateful display of anger, but a steady and determined opposition to all which violates the holiness, justice, and love of God. Put another way, we must never mistake divine wrath for human wrath, as is so often done. Indeed, the anger of humanity is often wild, animated, and vengeful — consumed in hateful passions that are anything but holy. God's anger, on the other hand, is not like this. Instead, it is a holy, loving, and determined opposition to all evil, to all which detracts from the honor and glory of love.

Interestingly enough, those who reject the notion of the wrath of God often do so in the name of love. They reason that the Almighty who is merciful, kind, and compassionate would never seriously punish the sinner and certainly not eternally. In this view, there can be no dire and lasting consequences to sin. Given these assumptions, which by the way lack the clear support of Scripture, God would have to, in effect, deny His own holy nature, reject justice and the moral order of the universe, and indulge sinners in their rebellion — and all of this in the name of love! But the question remains: Has the love of God been properly understood?

There is another side of this broken relationship which indicates why a mediator is necessary, and it has to do not with the

Godward side, the objective perspective, but with the humanward side, the subjective perspective. Unfortunately, in many treatments of the work of Christ as the Mediator between God and humanity, the offense against a holy God, the objective dimension, is often considered in depth, but the other side of the relation, the human element, in terms of both fear and a sinful distrust of God, is hardly treated at all. In such assessments, Jesus Christ is not really a *mediator* between God and humanity, because the human side of the relationship is never really taken seriously. Here the work of Christ *as a man* representing the race before an offended God is thoroughly explored, but little if any consideration is given to the *work of God* in Christ, reaching out sacrificially in love to reconcile a sinful and rebellious humanity.

On the other hand, a view which sees Jesus Christ as a true mediator between God and humanity can honestly and realistically take account of the reluctance of men and women to trust God, sinful as it is; it can reckon with the fear of God which has been left in sin's wake; and it can even consider the misplaced anger toward the Creator with a design, of course, to overcoming it. In other words, it is no one less than God who must act in Jesus Christ and demonstrate to humanity that it is He and He alone who is worthy of the love, honor, and trust of humanity. It is God, Himself, who must overcome human anger, fear, and distrust through the demonstration and power of His redeeming sacrifice. And it is God who must reach out to humanity in healing love if redemption is to occur. Accordingly, if God does not initiate, nothing will happen. Paul explores this saving activity of God in Christ in 2 Corinthians:

> All this is from God, who reconciled us to himself through Christ and gave us the ministry of reconciliation: that God was reconciling the world to himself in Christ, not counting men's sins against them. And he has committed to us the message of reconciliation (2 Cor. 5:18-19).

In summary, then, in light of the disruption of fellowship between God and humanity due to sin, what is needed from the objective perspective is a mediator who as a man can represent humanity before God, make satisfaction for sins, destroy the power and guilt of sin, and reaffirm the moral order in its integrity and righteousness. From the subjective perspective, however, what is needed is a mediator who is none other than God Himself who overcomes the alienation, fear, and distrust of fallen humanity through a display of humble, sacrificial love—a love which earnestly reaches out to fallen men and women, high and low, rich and poor, ever with the goal of reconciliation and communion. Again, it is precisely Jesus Christ, the God/Man, who is able to accomplish this work of redemption. It is He and He alone who is able to set the captives free: "For there is one God and one mediator between God and men, the man Christ Jesus, who gave himself as a ransom for all men—the testimony given in its proper time" (1 Tim. 2:5-6).

THE ATONEMENT

Having explored the necessity of a mediator between God and humanity, indicating why people are unable by their own efforts to overcome the potent realities of sin, evil, and guilt, we must now consider in greater detail the nature and extent of the work of the Mediator, the reconciliation which Christ has established between God and humanity, a work most often referred to as the atonement. In order to facilitate this discussion, we will explore four English terms which get at the heart of the atoning work of Christ, namely: propitiation, reconciliation, justification, and redemption.[3]

Propitiation

The first word which pertains to the atonement is propitiation, and it is utilized to translate the Greek nouns *hilasterios* and *hilasmos* as well as the verb *hilaskomai,* as the following verses from the *New American Standard Bible* indicate.

> Being justified as a gift by His grace through the redemption which is in Christ Jesus whom God displayed publicly as a **propitiation** *[hilasterios]* in His blood through faith. This was to demon-

strate His righteousness, because in the forbearance of God He passed over the sins previously committed (Rom. 3:24-25).

Therefore, He had to be made like His brethren in all things, that He might become a merciful and faithful high priest in things pertaining to God, to make **propitiation** *[hilaskomai]* for the sins of the people (Heb. 2:17).

He Himself is the **propitiation** *[hilasmos]* for our sins; and not for ours only, but also for those of the whole world (1 John 2:2).

In this is love, not that we loved God, but that He loved us and sent His Son to be the **propitiation** *[hilasmos]* for our sins (1 John 4:10).

Compare these same verses, however, with the translation of the *New International Version* where the Greek terms are not rendered by the English word "propitiation" but by another choice of words.

God presented him as a **sacrifice of atonement** *[hilasterios]*, through faith in his blood. He did this to demonstrate his justice, because in his forbearance he had left the sins committed beforehand unpunished (Rom. 3:25).

For this reason he had to be made like his brothers in every way, in order that he might become a merciful and faithful high priest in service to God, and that he might **make atonement** *[hilaskomai]* for the sins of the people (Heb. 2:17).

He is the **atoning sacrifice** *[hilasmos]* for our sins, and not only for ours but also for the sins of the whole world (1 John 2:2).

This is love: not that we loved God, but that he loved us and sent his Son as an **atoning sacrifice** *[hilasmos]* for our sins (1 John 4:10).

For some biblical scholars, then, it appears that the *New International Version* brings out the essential meaning of these passages in a clearer fashion than does the *New American Standard Bible* in the latter's preference for the term "propitiation"—a term which hardly communicates to English readers. Indeed, by translating *hilasterios* and its associated terms as "atoning sacrifice" or "sacrifice of atonement," the *New International Version* is able to highlight all the elements which are basic to understanding the redemptive work of Christ. Indeed, Christ's work as an "atoning sacrifice" indicates that He, as the mediator between God and humanity, has turned aside the *wrath of God,* which is rightly directed toward sinners, by sacrificing Himself as an offering to God. John Stott explains:

> What is revealed to us in Scripture is a pure doctrine . . . of God's holy wrath, his loving self-sacrifice in Christ and his initiative to avert his own anger. It is obvious that "wrath" and "propitiation" (the placating of wrath) go together.[4]

Here, in other words, the divine righteousness is satisfied by the One who acts on behalf of humanity. To be sure, integral to the idea of Christ as an atoning sacrifice is the notion of substitution, that Christ acts on our behalf and in a way which we could not. Truly, the heart of sin, as we have seen throughout, is humanity substituting itself for God, taking the role of the divine. We, therefore, should not be surprised to learn that the heart of redemption is just the opposite: God substituting Himself for humanity, taking its place, and bearing its guilt and condemnation.[5] Again, we had usurped the place of God through unbelief and pride; Jesus Christ, however, took our place as sinners in the deepest humility: "God made him who had no sin to be sin for us, so that in him we might become the righteousness of God" (2 Cor. 5:21).

Reconciliation

There are two key words—and one minor one—which the New Testament uses to communicate the idea of reconciliation. The first term, *apokatallass,* which means "to reconcile completely from," or "to change from one condition to another,"[6] is found in Colossians.

Once you were alienated from God and were enemies in your minds because of your evil behavior. But now he has reconciled *[apokatallass]* you by Christ's physical body through death to present you holy in his sight, without blemish and free from accusation (Col. 1:21-22).

In this context, it is apparent that reconciliation presupposes alienation between God and humanity due to sin. A separation definitely exists. As noted in passing earlier, this alienation, this enmity, must be considered from both sides of the relation: that is, God is "the enemy" of humanity due to the latter's sin, and humanity is the enemy of God due to unbelief and rebellion. The work of reconciliation, then, is the activity of God in Christ whereby He reconciles the world to Himself and thereby overcomes the estrangement which had once existed: "For God was pleased to have all his fullness dwell in him, and through him to reconcile *[apokatallass]* to himself all things, whether things on earth or things in heaven, by making peace through his blood shed on the cross" (Col. 1:19-20). Reconciliation, then, is at the heart of the idea of atonement, ever crucial to our understanding of "at-one-ment."

A second window on what the New Testament means by reconciliation is found in considering the Greek term *katallasso* and its derivatives which denote a change from enmity to friendship. In 2 Corinthians 5:19, for example, the Apostle Paul writes "that God was reconciling *[katallass]* the world to himself in Christ, not counting men's sins against them. And he has committed to us the message of reconciliation *[katallag]*." Observe in this passage three important truths: first, that God, not humanity, is the One who takes the initiative in reconciliation. He is the subject, in other words, the agent who brings about peaceable relations. Second, the life and death of Christ is the means, the vehicle, if you will, through which God accomplishes this reconciliation. And finally, the Apostle Paul reveals in this letter that men and women, those who embrace the glad tidings of salvation in Jesus Christ, are privileged to become the proclaimers, the ambassadors, of the elimination of the enmity between God and humanity.[7]

Justification

Since the righteous wrath of God has been placated by the sacrifice of Jesus Christ and since the integrity of the moral order has been upheld by the offering of the Son, the way is now clear to forgive people of their past sins and offenses against the Most High and to cleanse them from the pollution of sin and guilt. This act of God, based upon the atonement of Jesus Christ in declaring sinners to be just, is called justification and there is no proper Christian life without it.

In his epistles, Paul is insistent that the way to justification, the way to being declared righteous by God, is not by self-effort, not by an attempt to obey the law of God perfectly, but is received by grace through faith, a faith which trusts in Jesus Christ and which is united with his atoning benefit. The apostle explains:

> Know that a man is not justified *[dikaio]* by observing the law but by faith in Jesus Christ. So we, too, have put our faith in Christ Jesus that we may be justified by faith in Christ and not by observing the law, because by observing the law no one will be justified (Gal. 2:16).

Indeed, so emphatic was the Apostle Paul on this point that elsewhere he writes, "Clearly no one is justified before God by the law, because, 'The righteous will live by faith' " (Gal. 3:11).

Centuries later, during the Reformation, Martin Luther underscored that justification is by faith alone, *sola fide,* apart from works of the law. In his *Lectures on Romans* (1515), for example, he explores the "righteousness of men" and then, interestingly enough, distinguishes it from what is deemed righteousness in the sight of God, *coram Deo.* Luther explains:

> Human teachings reveal the righteousness of men, i.e., they teach who is righteous and how a man can be and become righteous before himself and his fellow men. But only the gospel reveals the righteousness of God. . . .[8]

This path to justification which both the Apostle Paul and Martin Luther have described is, no doubt, offensive and troubling to those who remain intent on justifying themselves through their good works, charitable deeds, belief in ideology, or through some other form of self-effort. In fact, this all-too-human approach toward justification, misguided as it is, constitutes the last attempt of the kingdom of self to maintain its power and rule. If the self can no longer live with the problem of sin and guilt, then it, itself, will solve this problem — and on its own terms. In this context, then, the sinful self arrogantly pretends that it is a master, not a servant, that it, not God, can reestablish the relationship that has been destroyed by sin. But this effort, as noble at times as it may seem, is futile for two key reasons. First of all, the way of the cross, God's gracious offer of redemption in Jesus Christ, reveals that humanity must approach God with nothing in its hands, and must, therefore, humbly receive His gracious offer of salvation in Jesus Christ, the One who comes to us and bridges the distance between God and humanity in love.

Second, the attempt at self-justification, the vain hope that humanity can make itself righteous, not only fails to consider that it is God, after all, who justifies ("Who will bring any charge against those whom God has chosen? It is God who justifies"; Rom. 8:33), but it also fails to note that the Almighty justifies not the righteous, not those who clean themselves up, so to speak, but sinners as Paul clearly states, "However, to the man who does not work but trusts God who justifies the wicked, his faith is credited as righteousness" (Rom. 4:5). Justification, then, is not a matter of humanity making itself fit and worthy to receive the forgiveness of God, as Kant had intimated in his book, *Religion within the Limits of Reason Alone,* but of humanity despairing of all self-effort and receiving God's gracious offer of salvation in Jesus Christ. Again, it is not a matter of reform, but of revolution, not a matter of self-help or actualization, but of facing away from the self and toward God. The difference is significant.

Given the nature of human sin with its unbelief, pride, and rebellion, it actually makes eminent sense that the way back to peace with God has to be by faith, a faith which humbles us, gets us outside ourselves and our sinful self-will, and directs us to God's saving activity in Jesus Christ. The source of forgiveness and justification, then, is not within ourselves, but is beyond us.

It is, as Luther said, an "alien righteousness," external to us. It is found at the cross. "Since we have now been justified by his blood," the Apostle Paul writes, "how much more shall we be saved from God's wrath through him!" (Rom. 5:9) Moreover, Leon Morris in his work, *The Apostolic Preaching of the Cross*, expresses this important truth well:

> The man who believes in Christ the propitiation — who stakes his whole being on sin-bearing love as the last reality in the universe — is not fictitiously regarded as right with God; he is actually right with God, and God treats him as such.[9]

Again, the way to the forgiveness of sins is not direct, as we had once supposed, but indirect; we must have faith in the mediator between God and humanity, Jesus Christ.

Redemption

Whereas the basis for justification underscores remission of guilt and the forgiveness of sins, the word "redemption" highlights the condition of sinful men and women — a condition from which they must be delivered. And in order to explore fully what the New Testament means by redemption, a term rich in so many ways, four leading themes will be taken into account.

First of all, redemption involves being "saved from" something. The gospel of Matthew, for instance, reveals that Christ "gave his life as a *ransom* for many" (20:28). In this context, then, the term "ransom" indicates that the Messiah has freed us from the bondage of sin and evil in which we were once held. He has liberated us, in other words, from the awful captivity, the slavery, of rebellion against God. In fact, the Greek word used in this particular verse is *lutron*, and it literally means "to loose" and in this instance "to loose away sin."

Moreover, *lutron* and its associated terms are not only behind the English word "ransom," as used in the New Testament, but they are behind the term "redemption" as well. The verb *lutro*, for instance, basically means "to redeem, to release on receipt of ransom,"[10] and it is found in Titus 2:14: "Jesus Christ, who gave himself for us to redeem us *[lutro]* from all wickedness and to purify for himself a people that are his very own, eager to do what is good." Again, notice the emphasis on "saving from," in this context that Christ is able to deliver us from all manner of wickedness — from the powers of evil, sin, and darkness, from all that oppresses the human spirit.

Another term which the New Testament uses to convey the idea of deliverance, of salvation from the power of sin, is *apolutrosis,* and it is employed about ten times in all. On occasion, this term is translated as "redemption," as in Romans 3:24, but other times it appears as "ransom," as in Hebrews 9:15: "For this reason Christ is the mediator of a new covenant, that those who are called may receive the promised eternal inheritance — now that he has died as a ransom to set them free from the sins committed under the first covenant." Where human power was conquered by evil, Christ has triumphed and liberated; where human power was weak, Christ has remained strong; what the first covenant could not do by the law, Christ has done by grace.

One last term which the New Testament uses to underscore the notion of "salvation from" in the idea of redemption is *exagoraz.* Interestingly enough, this verb is an intensified form of *agorazo* which literally means "to buy out, especially of purchasing a slave with a view to his freedom."[11] In his letter to the Galatians, for example, the Apostle Paul writes: "Christ redeemed *[exagoraz]* us from the curse of the law by becoming a curse for us" (Gal. 3:13). Jesus Christ, then, has not only freed us from the shackles of sin, He has not only served as our substitute by bearing the curse which, rightfully speaking, we should have borne, but He has also purchased us for God. Jesus Christ, then, has paid the price and liberated us from the prison house of sin.

The second theme which informs the New Testament concept of redemption is the idea of "being saved to" something. Indeed, the "negative work" of being *saved from* sin must be complemented by the "positive work" of being *saved to* a qualitatively distinct kind of life, a life of purity and love. To illustrate, in exploring what is implied in the work of redemption, Paul writes of "giving thanks to the Father, who has qualified you to share in the inheritance of the saints in the kingdom of light" (Col. 1:12). Beyond this, in the gospel of Luke, Jesus encourages believers at the end of the age "to stand up and lift up your heads, because your redemption *[apolutrosis]* is near" (Luke 21:28). And though these references are obviously to the future, it would be a mistake to conclude that the new life to which we are called is only a future reality and not a present one. Clearly, both the Apostle Paul and the Apostle John have taken great care in their writings to demonstrate that the present power of redemption, which, no doubt, has future consequences, is available to all those who trust in Jesus Christ.

The third theme of redemption has to do with the cost of deliverance, the price which Jesus Christ paid to ransom people from their sins and to redeem them to a life of holy love. Scripture explores this cost in two key ways: first of all, there are those passages which specifically reveal that the price of redemption is nothing less than the life of Christ. The author of Hebrews, for instance, writes: "But now he [Christ] has appeared once for all at the end of the ages to do away with sin by the *sacrifice of himself*" (Heb. 9:26). And again, in 1 Timothy 2:6, we observe that Christ "gave *himself* as a ransom for all men." Christ's whole being, his very life, was the price of salvation.

Beyond this, there are those passages, several in number, which symbolically point to the blood of Christ as the price of salvation. In 1 Peter 1:18-19 the author exclaims: "For you know that it was not with perishable things such as silver or gold that you were redeemed from the empty way of life handed down to you from your forefathers, but with the precious blood of Christ, a lamb without blemish or defect." Elsewhere, Paul writes: "In him [Christ] we have redemption through his blood, the forgiveness of sins, in accordance with the riches of God's grace" (Eph. 1:7). The appeal to the blood of Christ in these passages, then, not only indicates that the offering of the life of Messiah constitutes the price of redemption, but it also highlights, in a way the earlier passages did not, that it is more specifically the *death* of Christ which liberates.

And finally, implicit in the New Testament understanding of redemption is the idea that the Redeemer, the one who has sacrificed and offered His life as a ransom to set the captives free, has "proprietary rights over his purchase."[12] Accordingly, though at one time we belonged to sin and evil, now through grace, we can belong to God. Christ has purchased our lives by paying the price of redemption. Whereas once we were slaves to sin, now we can become slaves to righteousness. The Apostle Paul explains:

> And you also were included in Christ when you heard the word of truth, the gospel of your salvation. Having believed, you were marked in him with a seal, the promised Holy Spirit, who is a deposit guaranteeing our inheritance until the redemption [*apolutrosis*] of those who are God's possession — to the praise of his glory (Eph. 1:13-14).

In a real sense, then, we can never actually be independent as we once had mistakenly supposed. The self-rule of the kingdom of self was an illusion. One way or the other, we will be the servants of a master. We will either be the servants of sin which leads to guilt and condemnation or we will be the servants of God which leads to righteousness and peace. Again, we will either be held captive to sin in unbelief, pride, and self-will, or we will belong to God in Jesus Christ through faith.

The Cross as the Revelation of Divine, Healing Love

Though it is helpful to explore Christ's work on behalf of sinners in terms of the four key words noted above, and though the preceding material has considered both the objective as well as some of the subjective aspects of the Atonement, the latter aspect nevertheless still needs further development if a thorough and satisfactory view is to emerge. Clearly, the subjective and personal changes which take place in the human heart due to the display of the love of God at Calvary must be considered at this point, for the work of God in Christ is not merely external to us, but must also become a vital part of our inner being with transforming power.

A medieval theologian who explored this subjective dimension in great detail was Peter Abelard, abbot of the monastery of St. Gildas-de-Rhuys in Brittany during the twelfth century. And though Abelard's emphasis in his doctrine of the Atonement was obviously different from that of Anselm, who had emphasized the so-called "objective elements," there is nothing which prevents the harmonization of these two teachings in a larger, more inclusive whole. For one thing, Abelard's work, which is sometimes referred to as the moral influence theory, directs us to a consideration of the person of Christ and to the effect which His sacrificial death has on the human heart — important elements in any consideration of the salvation of humanity.

Before we explore these other aspects of the atoning work of Christ, a few comments must be made about the nature of the language we will employ. In the material above, it was appropriate to use intellectual concepts and a few abstractions to communicate the external aspects of the Atonement, of how Christ, for example, was our substitute, ransomed us, and became the basis for our justification. Such a discussion was, no doubt, necessary for any serious view of the work of Christ; nevertheless, abstract, intellectual language is not able by itself to communicate the full richness of the redemptive work of Jesus. Indeed, if this language is not supplemented by a different kind, as well as by some other considerations, we will run the risk of conceiving salvation *merely* as an intellectual exercise, a speculative thing, utterly external to us, where the work of Christ has consequence only for our thought, but not for our hearts as well.

More to the point, even a cursory reading of the gospels will convince the average reader that these narratives seek to address not simply the human mind, but the whole person: body, mind, and spirit. In light of this, we too must utilize another form of language, a different rhetoric, just as the gospels do, in order to communicate the full bounty, the richness, of the redemptive work of Christ. The appeal here, then, will be principally not to theoretical concepts and language, though these are important, but to story. In fact, the language of story or narrative is the chief vehicle which the gospels use to communicate some of their deepest truths. Indeed, the gospel stories have an uncanny way of drawing us into their world and of inviting us to become a participant in a larger drama. Story, in other words, can move us in a way that concepts cannot; it can touch us at the deepest recesses of our being; it can address the whole person.

The Crucifixion of Christ

Toward the goal of displaying the fullness of the work of Christ, we will consider Matthew's account of the Crucifixion, and we will pay particular attention not only to the event itself, but also to some of the observations made by the religious leaders whose actions led to the death of Jesus. Such an approach should issue in a better understanding of the death of Christ and its consequence for all men and women, from whatever time, place, or culture.

First of all, the crucifixion of Jesus Christ must be viewed not simply as an isolated event, but in terms of His larger public ministry and the latter's effect on both the religious leaders of Israel as well as the common people. All the gospel narratives, for instance, are in agreement that the popularity of Jesus increased throughout His ministry and, more importantly for the task at hand, that this favor with the masses in some way contributed to His death. In particular, by the time Jesus made His triumphal entry into Jerusalem amidst cries of "Blessed is he who comes in the name of the Lord" (Matt. 21:9), the religious leaders of Israel were already determined to put a stop to this engaging, traveling preacher. Motivated by jealousy and intent on preserving their own popularity with the people ("If we let him go on like this, everyone will believe in him, and then the Romans will come and take away both *our* place and *our* nation," John 11:48), the Sanhedrin charged Jesus with nothing less than blasphemy for claiming to be the Son of God and they, therefore, sought His death.

But the religious leaders had a problem. Since they were under Roman rule, a rule which they despised, they did not have the authority to execute Jesus themselves, and so they turned Him over to Pontius Pilate, the Roman governor of Judea. To the charge of blasphemy — for which Pilate cared nothing — they added the offense of sedition, that Jesus had proclaimed Himself a King and was therefore in rebellion against Caesar. Interrogated by Pilate, who found Him innocent, mocked and beaten by soldiers, Jesus was eventually led out to be crucified.

Though there are many passages from the gospels which portray the love of God manifest at the cross very clearly, the following is perhaps the most revealing. Among other things it places Jesus in sharp contrast to the rulers of the Jews. Matthew elaborates:

> Two robbers were crucified with him, one on his right and one on his left. Those who passed by hurled insults at him, shaking their heads and saying, "You who are going to destroy the temple and build it in three days, save yourself! Come down from the cross, if you are the Son of God!" In the same way the chief priests, the teachers of the law and the elders mocked him. "He saved others," they said, "but he can't save himself! He's the King of Israel! Let him come down now from the cross, and we will believe in him. He trusts in God. Let God rescue him now if he wants him, for he said, 'I am the Son of God.' " In the same way the robbers who were crucified with him also heaped insults on him (Matt. 27:38-44).

If we were eyewitnesses to this event and familiar with the ministry of Jesus of Nazareth, surely we would ask ourselves: "How did such a man end up like this, nailed to a tree, mocked, despised and rejected, and with a criminal on either side of him?" For which of His good works was he being put to death? Was it because he took compassion on people and fed the hungry, healed the sick, and raised the dead? Was it because he proclaimed a Gospel of hope for the downtrodden and brokenhearted? Or was it because he so loved God, whom He called His Father, that He was willing to suffer any burden to bring good news to the poor in spirit? For which of these good deeds, then, was Jesus of Nazareth condemned? Indeed, in all of human history, there never was nor will there ever be a more unjust act as when Jesus of Nazareth, the One who committed no evil, the only human being who was truly innocent, was put to death.

Moreover, not only did Jesus suffer the pain of scourging, the cruelty of the Roman soldiers, the agony and humiliation of crucifixion — as if these things were not enough to satisfy the wild and irrational hatred which placed Him on the cross — but He was also taunted by the passersby, first by the common people and then by the religious leaders themselves. Matthew tells us, for instance, that in the midst of the cruelties of that day those who walked by the cross hurled insults at Jesus and challenged Him to save Himself: "Come down from the cross, if you are the Son of God," they cried (Matt. 27:40). For these mockers, then, the Son of God must have nothing to do with rejection, suffering, and death; He must, in other words, be rid of the cross. A Messiah who suffers, who sacrifices Himself on behalf of the people was simply an abomination to their way of thinking. But what would it have been like if the passersby had thought of Jesus not in terms of their own assumptions and prejudices, but in terms of the words of the Prophet Isaiah:

> He was despised and rejected by men, a man of sorrows, and familiar with suffering. Like one from whom men hide their faces he was despised, and we esteemed him not. Surely he took up our infirmities and carried our sorrows, yet we considered him stricken by God, smitten by him, and afflicted.
>
> But he was pierced for our transgressions, he was crushed for our iniquities; the punishment that brought us peace was upon him, and by his wounds we are healed.
>
> We all, like sheep, have gone astray, each of us has turned to his own way; and the Lord has laid on him the iniquity of us all.
>
> He was oppressed and afflicted, yet he did not open his mouth; he was led like a lamb to the slaughter, and as a sheep before her shearers is silent, so he did not open his mouth. By oppression and judgment he was taken away. And who can speak of his descendants? For he was cut off from the land of the living; for the transgression of my people he was stricken.
>
> He was assigned a grave with the wicked, and with the rich in his death, though he had done no violence, nor was any deceit in his mouth. Yet it was the Lord's will to crush him and cause him to suffer, and though the Lord makes his life a guilt offering, he will see his offspring and prolong his days, and the will of the Lord will prosper in his hand.
>
> After the suffering of his soul, he will see the light [of life] and be satisfied; by his knowledge my righteous servant will justify many, and he will bear their iniquities. Therefore I will give him a portion among the great, and he will divide the spoils with the

strong, because he poured out his life unto death, and was num-
bered with the transgressors. For he bore the sin of many, and
made intercession for the transgressors (Isa. 53:3-12).[13]

Soon the religious leaders added their voices to the crowd and
taunted Jesus in a number of ways, giving full evidence of their
cruelty. First of all, the chief priests ridiculed Christ by saying:
" 'He saved others . . . but he can't save himself!' " (Matt. 27:42)
But there is irony here, for what was originally meant to be an
indictment against Jesus actually turns out to be an indictment
against the religious leaders themselves. Notice, for instance, the
hypocrisy of the chief priests and the teachers of the law who
admitted that Jesus, after all, "saved others" (Matt. 27:42), yet
they still refused to believe in Him. Furthermore, should a man
who has, in fact, saved others come to such an end as this? Was
this appropriate? Was this just? Unfortunately, the man who had
preached, "love your enemies," was being put to death by His.
Jealousy and hatred would have it no other way.

Second, the Pharisees and Saducees, in a similar fashion to the
common people before them, scoffed at Jesus: "He's the King of
Israel! Let him come down now from the cross, and we will
believe in him" (Matt. 27:42). Observe the kind of person that
these leaders associate with being the king of Israel. In their
minds, at least, the king must not be lowly and humble, and he
must never descend to a low, abject state of human existence,
but should free himself through some sort of miracle or divine
intervention. Their taunt, then, was a demand not to identify with
some of the meanest elements in life, and in this particular case
with two robbers, but to be as respectable as the religious leaders
thought themselves to be.

But Jesus chose another way. In His crucifixion and death, He
identified with all people, from the highest to the lowest, from
the most esteemed to the most despised. His identification in
love was so thorough that there was not a man or woman whom
He could not touch. As the King of Israel, Jesus could relate to
the very highest; as the Messiah, as the suffering servant, He
could identify with the very lowest, with all those who were
under the bondage of evil. In fact, the self-surrender of Jesus on

the cross, His abandonment to the lowest depths of human existence, constitutes the real work of the Messiah as the one who spans the gulf of separation between God and humanity. The alienation between a holy God and the worst of sinners had finally been overcome. In light of this, the request of the religious leaders was, in effect, an odd one, for they were asking God's anointed One not to redeem all of humanity, but only a select few. The "respectable" and "virtuous" might be saved, but certainly not contemptible sinners. They wanted God's grace, in other words, to stop at their level and to go no further.

Beyond this, it is clear by their comments around the cross that the Pharisees and Saducees did not understand what is meant by real power. For them, the only power which was apparently valuable was the kind which could remove Jesus from the cross and which could liberate Him from suffering, shame, and disgrace. However, there was a much different kind of power displayed at Calvary, and the religious leaders failed to see it. For after all that was done to Jesus on the day of His death—the flogging, the crucifixion, the mocking and taunting—He still loved his enemies: "Father, forgive them, for they do not know what they are doing" (Luke 23:34). Again, the power of Jesus is not like other power; it is not coercive but engaging; it does not force its will on anyone, but invites; it does not avoid the onslaught of evil, but bears all things in order to overcome them in love. The love of Jesus Christ was, is, and will always be unconquerable. Nails cannot destroy it; flogging cannot weaken it; hatred cannot overcome it. It is a love which is eternal. All this and more was missed in the mockery of the religious leaders; all this was lost in their spiteful taunts.

The last gibe of the religious leaders came in the form: "He trusts in God. Let God rescue him now if he wants him" (Matt. 27:43). Once again observe the hypocrisy. In the first part of this statement the chief priests and teachers of the law freely admit that Jesus trusts in God, and yet they sought His death. In the second part of their taunt, these same leaders maintain that in order for Christ to be the Savior, He should by no means give His all, His very life, for the sake of humanity; instead, He should think only of Himself, save His own life, and forget others—just as they would do if they were in his place. Again, these leaders failed to understand that it is a sacrificial Lamb who would redeem, that lowliness and humility—so despised by the world—would triumph over hatred, mocking, and shame. Compare the counsel of the Pharisees and Saducees with the insight which Paul shows concerning the death of Christ.

> Your attitude should be the same as that of Christ Jesus: Who, being in very nature God, did not consider equality with God something to be grasped, but made himself nothing, taking the very nature of a servant, being made in human likeness. And being found in appearance as a man, he humbled himself and became obedient to death—even death on a cross! Therefore God exalted him to the highest place and gave him the name that is above every name, that at the name of Jesus every knee should bow, in heaven and on earth and under the earth, and every tongue confess that Jesus Christ is Lord, to the glory of God the Father (Phil. 2:5-11).

Truly, the "weakness" of God is far more powerful than the strength of humanity, and the "foolishness" of the cross is far wiser than the wisdom of men and women. As Paul notes, God gave His all for us in Christ so that we could be liberated from the power of sin, guilt, and evil. And as Irenaeus stated long ago: "For the sake of His infinite love He has become what we are in order that He may make us entirely what He is." A self-concerned Messiah, then, one who would redeem himself above all, one who would come down from the cross, would be no Messiah at all.

THE RECEPTION OF THE POWER OF THE CROSS

Grace and Faith

It is no mistake that many of the great spiritual classics, such as *The Spiritual Exercises of St. Ignatius,* make the passion and death of Christ their chief point of attention. To be sure, it is when we hear a clear proclamation of the good news of the Gospel, that Christ died not for the righteous but for sinners, that the cold-

ness and frigidity of the kingdom of self begins to melt away
through the gracious activity of the Holy Spirit. Comprehending
for the first time what the love of Christ entails, appreciating His
sacrifice, our souls are moved and transformed in a number of
ways. First of all, knowing that Christ stood in our place at Calvary and bore a just and righteous judgment, we are no longer
afraid to approach the Most High. Unlike Adam and Eve who hid
themselves in the garden, we are now free to come out into the
open, to enjoy the light of fellowship. Through the work of
Christ, the new Adam, the author of a new humanity, the God we
once feared has become the God we now love: "We love because
He first loved us" (1 John 4:19).

Moreover, understanding that on the basis of Christ's sacrificial death, God declares us justified, we can receive God's saving
offer of forgiveness through faith and thereby be set free from
the gnawing power of guilt. It doesn't matter what evil we have
committed in the past or how long we have committed it; God's
forgiveness is greater. Christ has paid *all* the penalty; He has
plumbed the depths of human existence and borne it all. What
once held us captive has now lost its sting through the power of
the cross. Trusting in Jesus Christ, then, we can have the assurance that our sins have been forgiven, that all our past acts of
wickedness have been wiped away. Our consciences need not
plague us any longer for it is no one less than God Himself who
declares us righteous.

Third, believing that Jesus Christ is our Redeemer, the One
who ransoms us from the destructive powers which once over-
whelmed us, we can be free not simply from the guilt of sin, but
from its very power as well. And this is truly a remarkable
victory. What we could not do by our own efforts, God has done
by His grace. By being united to Christ through faith, His
power becomes our power, His victory is our victory. A pessimism of nature, which had dominated our old way of thinking,
"we're only human," is transformed into an optimism of grace, "I
can do everything through him who gives me strength" (Phil.
4:13).

Fourth, trusting that Christ has borne the wrath which was
rightfully ours due to sin, knowing that God through the work of

the Mediator has forgiven our sins, we can receive, through the gracious ministry of the Holy Spirit, the gift of reconciliation. Where once there was turmoil, now there is peace. And this reconciliation between God and humanity which we experience in our hearts is also manifested toward our neighbors. As reconciled people, we are free to relate to others in a new way. Since we have been forgiven so much, we genuinely want to forgive others. Moreover, our erstwhile judgmental attitude toward our neighbor has been tempered by the reality of the cross; that is, we see unrepentant sinners as being in exactly the same condition in which we once were: alienated from God's love due to unbelief, and turned toward self in sinful pride. Here, then, is an opportunity for compassion and understanding, an occasion to bear with the evil and shortcomings of others just as God has borne ours.

The Call to Discipleship

The sacrificial love of Christ at the cross has finally shown the kingdom of self for what it is: weak, insecure, and shameful. Who will now stand up for disobedience against God, when Jesus obeyed the Father unto death, even death on a cross? Who will champion unswerving self-interest, looking out for number one, when Christ gave all that He had for others? And who will exalt pride and arrogance, when the Messiah was meek and lowly in heart, gentle in soul, the One who identified with sinners in their state of utter dejection? To be sure, in the face of the cross which, magnificently displays both God's love for humanity and the awful reality of human evil, the kingdom of self now looks quite ugly, a mean thing, an aberration in the universe that was never meant to be.

Moreover, the transition from the kingdom of self to the kingdom of God, the abandonment of self-rule for the rule of the Almighty, raises the prospect and necessity of being a lifelong disciple of Jesus Christ, of being truly dead to our old way of life. Indeed, as justified and regenerated believers, we have been crucified with Christ: "For we know that our old self was crucified with him so that the body of sin might be done away with, that we should no longer be slaves to sin" (Rom. 6:6). Accordingly,

Christ's death has become our death, but not in the sense that we bear the burdens of sin, but in the sense that in Christ we have died to the old sinful self. This means, of course, that the kingdom of self must remain vacant; it must be a realm without a monarch; its ruler has died. Truly, we belong to another kingdom, even the kingdom of God.

But discipleship has not only to do with dying to self, but also with living to God. As children who are born of God, we share in Christ's resurrection. His life has now become our life and He lives within us through the power of the Holy Spirit. Having been liberated from sinful pride and excessive self-concern, we are free to enjoy the fruits of love, of reaching out to our neighbors in mercy and compassion. Having the newly awakened assurance of God's love, we are strengthened inwardly. Who we are as people, our very identities, are no longer subject to the whims and tastes of the crowd, in bondage to their approval or disapproval. Instead, we take our security, our strength, and our very being in knowing that we are the children of God. And having the hope of being with God forever, we do not set our hearts on any worldly thing ("May I never boast except in the cross of our Lord Jesus Christ, through which the world has been crucified to me, and I to the world," Gal. 6:14) but we set them on God and the love which He has manifested in Jesus Christ.

Our journey then from sin to grace, from disobedience and despair to faithfulness and hope, from self-absorption to compassion has, no doubt, been difficult. The straight and narrow is, after all, an arduous path, and anyone who tells you otherwise is mistaken. Nevertheless, the pain and struggles of spiritual growth are much to be preferred over the pain of alienation from God, the source of all life. The loosing of the shackles of self-centeredness is far better than the false and fleeting happiness of those who make themselves the monarchs of their own lives. The freedom to love, which has become a reality through faith in God, is far greater than the bondage of miserly self-rule. And in the end, if we are sensitive and wise enough, if we are patient with ourselves and take time to reflect on our journey, we will finally realize that all of this has been for love; it has all been for love.

SUMMING UP

In this chapter we have indicated why, due to human sin and evil, a direct approach to God is no longer possible. Therefore, a mediator between God and humanity is necessary—one who can both satisfy the righteousness of God as well as overcome humanity's fear of and rebellion against a holy God. Beyond this, we have highlighted the cross of Christ as the place where divine, sacrificial, healing love is most amply displayed.

In the next chapter we will set forth some of the more important disciplines of the Christian life which, through divine grace, can help us to abide in the kingdom of God.

INDIVIDUAL OR GROUP REFLECTION QUESTIONS

1 Why is a mediator necessary in dealing with the problem of sin and evil against God? Why can't we go directly to God ourselves, and why can't the moral law mediate this relationship? What, then, should be our relation to the mediator?

2 Does Christianity deal realistically with the problem of evil? Does evil have existence or is it an illusion? Is it ultimately real? Moreover, how does Christianity's response to this problem differ from that of other major world religions such as Hinduism and Buddhism?

3 Compare and contrast Anselm and Abelard's view of the Atonement. What are the strengths of each? What are their weaknesses? Can the two views be combined in a single doctrine? If so, what would the doctrine look like?

4 In the Christian doctrine of salvation, what are we saved from? What are we saved to? Why is not only justification but also the new birth necessary in order to live the kind of life to which God has called us? Put another way, why is the forgiveness of sins (justification) by itself not enough to meet the needs of the sinner? Why must there also be the work of regeneration (the new birth)?

5 Think of ways that you would use to communicate the Gospel to someone who is suffering under the power of evil. What methods would be appropriate? Which would be inappropriate? Would some ways of communicating make the listener defensive? Would other ways open him or her up? And finally, would it be wise to talk about ourselves or the other person in this encounter?

SEVEN

ABIDING IN THE KINGDOM OF GOD:

The Disciplines of the Liberated Life, Part I

For me, prayer means launching out of the heart towards God; it means lifting up one's eyes, quite simply, to Heaven, a cry of grateful love from the crest of joy on the trough of despair; it's a vast, supernatural force which opens out my heart, and binds me close to Jesus" (Thérèse De Lisieux).

The great transformation in our lives which takes place as a result of faith in Christ as our Savior and Lord involves not only the new perspective which comes from living from a much larger circle of meaning, but it also entails significant value change. Theologians refer to this dynamic more technically as "transvaluation." Simply put, transvaluation means that from our new vantage point of faith in Christ, some things we once cherished are no longer meaningful, while other things which we had previously neglected are now given great weight. Success, winning, "making it," and fulfillment all have new meanings.

Though popular American culture often parades the wonders of independence and self-actualization in many ways, the New Testament never holds up autonomous, independent, self-actualized human beings as the goal of life. In fact, the judgment of Scripture is so radically different from our normal way of thinking that we are most likely to misunderstand its teaching or even to reject it outright when we initially encounter it. That is, from the

Bible's vantage point, *all* human beings, not merely the obviously immoral, are slaves of some sort or other: from the Wall Street executive to the housewife, from the civic leader to the threatening robber, from the statesman to the political rebel, all serve a master. The difference, however, is that some serve other masters, but no one is without a master. As Bob Dylan's post-conversion anthem reminded us, "you gotta serve somebody." Utter freedom and independence, the claim that human beings are their own masters and the lord of their own lives, is an illusion. The Apostle Paul confirms this quite well.

> Don't you know that when you offer yourselves to someone to obey him as slaves, you are slaves to the one whom you obey — whether you are slaves to sin, which leads to death, or to obedience, which leads to righteousness? But thanks be to God that, though you used to be slaves to sin, you wholeheartedly obeyed the form of teaching to which you were entrusted. You have been set free from sin and have become slaves to righteousness (Rom. 6:16-18).

Again, the New Testament maintains that a person outside the rule of Christ is not free, but is actually a slave of sin *(doulos tes harmartias)*. Accordingly, self-will, which can appear to be so good, even an angel of light, must never be confused with liberation. In other words, giving people more of what they want and when they want it does not necessarily result in freedom, but may issue in yet greater bondage. Indeed, feeding self-will, however justified, may set up the tyranny of self from which arises jealousy, revenge, lust, class-hatred, and many other ungodly passions. Outside of Christ, then, there exists not liberty, as the world claims, but a kingdom of slavery, no matter how "dressed up" such slavery is. Colin Brown elaborates:

> This slavery is that of sin, i.e. man's obsession with the illusion that he can make or maintain his own life and freedom with reference only to himself and in his own power. That which the Greeks regarded as the highest form of freedom becomes in the NT the source of man's most abject bondage. Man, bent in upon himself,

obstinately waves God's help aside and busies himself in running his own life in his own strength, trusting in his own resources, and falls into the grip of fear.[1]

On the other hand—and this may offend the modern mentality as well—the New Testament uses the very same word *doulos* to describe a believer's proper relation to Christ. The Apostle Paul, for instance, in his opening remarks in Romans writes: "Paul a servant of Christ Jesus [Paulos *doulos* Christou Iesou], called to be an apostle" (Rom. 1:1). Moreover, in his letter to the universal church, James exclaims: "James, a servant of God [*doulos* Theou] and of the Lord Jesus Christ" (James 1:1). And in a similar fashion, Peter introduces his second epistle with the following salutation: "Simon Peter, a servant and apostle of Jesus Christ [*doulos* kai apostolos Iesou Christou]" (2 Peter 1:1). However, as Vine points out, in this present context the word *doulos*—which can be translated either as "slave" or "servant"—does indeed indicate subjection but without the idea of bondage.[2] The difference is important.

So then, the Christian community is composed of all those men and women who have, through grace and faith, subjected their own wills and lives to the direction and lordship of Christ, which is precisely what discipleship requires. This subjection, however, does not issue in bondage, as is mistakenly supposed by nominal Christianity and our secular society, but it brings the greatest liberty of all: freedom *from* the power and guilt of sin as well as the freedom *to* love God and neighbor, unfettered by excessive self-love. Simply put, from the Bible's perspective to be free from God is bondage; to be a servant (slave) of God is liberation. "Do you know when people really become spiritual?" Teresa of Ávila writes in her classic *Interior Castle*. "It is when they become the slaves of God and are branded with His sign, which is the sign of the cross."[3]

Discipleship, then, the *ongoing* submission of our wills and lives to Jesus Christ, will naturally entail a number of disciplines. Without them, we may slowly drift back to the shores of unbelief, pride, and even open sin. Indeed, the universal church is in agreement—Roman Catholicism, Eastern Orthodoxy, and Protestantism — that the carnal nature, with a propensity to backsliding, though it does not reign, still remains even in the life of the believer. Put another way, the graces of justification and regeneration, though they mark a significant advance in spiritual development, have not cleansed the heart of original sin. The enemy of all goodness, the old Adam, is in chains, but he still remains, and he desires to rule once again. This means, of course, that the Christian life must be one of ongoing vigilance, of a day-by-day, and at times of a moment-by-moment dependence on the sustaining grace of God. Original sin in the form of unbelief, rebellion, and the kingdom of self is ever willing and waiting once again to take control of human life. Not surprisingly, Paul, always concerned about the spiritual health of the church, sets up an analogy which explores the importance of discipline for the Christian life in one of his letters:

> Do you not know that in a race all the runners run, but only one gets the prize? Run in such a way as to get the prize. Everyone who competes in the games goes into strict training. They do it to get a crown that will not last; but we do it to get a crown that will last forever (1 Cor. 9:24-26).

Spiritual disciplines will be needed throughout our journey, for although we have received sanctifying grace, temptations and trials will never cease. But there is, however, an important difference between our earlier condition and our present state. We no longer have to face such troubles alone or in our own strength. As newly born sons and daughters of God, we now have the Holy Spirit with us, cleansing our hearts by faith, strengthening us inwardly, and comforting us when we are sorely pressed. Consequently, the three major disciplines which will be described in this chapter and the next are not attempts at self-effort, but constitute a serious response to the grace of God already received in justification and regeneration. They do not establish the Christian life, but they do provide the proper setting in which that life can flourish. In short, they are means of further grace, aids for our maturation, the vehicles through which we can receive the satisfying bounty of God.

PERSONAL DISCIPLINES

Personal, corporate, and public disciplines constitute the major activities of the Christian life. In particular, the personal disciplines, the major concern of this chapter, are characterized by diverse activities which, although they also take place within the context of the church, are often practiced by individuals alone. Put another way, reading the Scriptures, practicing devotional reading, praying and fasting, practices which make up the personal disciplines, often occur in the privacy of our homes, in our "prayer closet," or in the silence of our hearts. Moreover, these disciplines not only orient us toward God in a rich and personal way, and thereby develop the divine/human relationship, but they also prepare us to participate in the larger community of faith (corporate disciplines) and the world (public disciplines). And it is to these personal disciplines that we now turn.

Reading the Scriptures

It was Karl Barth, in one of his earlier theological essays, who talked about "the strange new world within the Bible."[4] Part of that strangeness which this leading Swiss theologian found in the Scriptures has to do, no doubt, with the "otherness" of God and His kingdom: that is, God's ways, as we've noted earlier, are not as our ways, and the kingdom of heaven — to use my own idiom — is so unlike the kingdom of self. It makes eminent sense, then, for those who are just embarking on the Christian life, as well as for those who are more spiritually mature, to read the Bible on a regular basis, to enter into that strange new world, and to identify not with self-interest but with the Word of God.

Beyond this, the attitude or the frame of mind which we bring to the Bible is significant. Though a higher-critical reading is both necessary and valuable in terms of understanding the historical context of the Scriptures, its various literary forms, as well as questions which pertain to authorship, date, and intended audience, a devotional reading is also necessary for significant growth in grace. Again, it is not a matter of one reading to the exclusion of the other, but of both readings in harmony with and complementing each other. In fact, if a higher-critical reading of the

Bible, which places human reason as the chief arbiter of all matters, is not supplemented by a devotional reading which allows our entire being (including our reason) to be addressed and called into account by the voice of God present in the Scriptures, then we may never hear God's call on our lives at all. Great care and earnestness, then, is called for here, a balance of reason and faith, an intellectual knowledge of the Scriptures on the one hand as well as greater personal and existential depth on the other.

Since the Christian community throughout the ages has affirmed that the Bible is the Word of God, an expression of the Almighty's most holy will, it is vitally important for us not only to read the Scriptures in their entirety, but also to study them in considerable depth. Three approaches are particularly helpful here. *First* of all, we should set up a daily reading program which will take us through the entire Bible, the Old Testament and the New, in about a year. After this, the cycle can be repeated with an eye to the improvement of the grace already received. Indeed, because the Scriptures are so rich in meaning, and also because we, ourselves, will grow from year to year, our reading of the Bible should never become stale but always remain fresh.

Second, when we read the Scriptures, we must not only master the elements of the story and the details of the historical record, keeping our Jehoiakims distinguished from our Jehoiachins, but we must also discern the larger moral and spiritual truths which are communicated by means of these historical accounts as an important step in our reading strategy. Here a good commentary on the Bible can be very useful in drawing out the truths of the text which we would have otherwise missed. But since commentaries often represent a particular viewpoint — whether it be Lutheran, Reformed, or Methodist — it is perhaps best to consult several different commentaries whose differences in interpretation will then force us to go back to the text in order to grapple with its meaning. Indeed, commentaries, though helpful, should never be a substitute for our own wrestling with the Scriptures.

The *third* and perhaps most important aspect of our reading of the Bible, and one which is often neglected in seminary and graduate courses, is the task of applying the truths which we have learned from our study of the Word of God to our lives and then to our communities. This practical application of the Bible means that we will not simply come to know its truths cognitively or intellectually, but that we will also endeavor, through the grace of God, to have these truths become a part of our person, a part of our lives and our communities with transforming power.

Sadly, due to our intellectual cultural heritage, we are so accustomed to thinking of the word "truth" as a noun, as a thing, or as a fact, when the larger truths of the Bible are best understood as action words and relations. Put another way, we live out the truths of the Bible; we participate in their reality; and our lives, then, become one of the many testaments to their being. Indeed, God is not a thing at all, as we had once supposed, an object which we can manipulate or control; instead, the essence, the very being, of God is one of *relation:* Father, Son, and Holy Spirit in eternal love—a love which reaches out to us and invites us to enjoy a much higher kind of life, a life which engages all aspects of our being.

Devotional Reading: The Import of Tradition

Besides the use of commentaries to explore the meaning of Scripture, it is helpful to engage in spiritual or devotional reading. For the most part, commentaries (depending on their publication date) will give us a contemporary view of the Bible; devotional readings, on the other hand, will acquaint us with the rich spiritual *tradition* of the universal church. By way of comparison, Mortimer Adler, philosopher and champion of the Great Books series, has talked about participating in the "great conversation"—a conversation which has been occurring in the West for thousands of years. Its participants range from the pre-Socratic philosophers such as Thales, Anaxamander, and Anaxamenes to such modern figures as Locke, Newton, and Marx. And in order to engage in this conversation with any seriousness, Adler argues, it is necessary to become acquainted with the writings of these leading figures. In a similar fashion, there is a great conversation which has been taking place during the nearly 2,000 years of Christianity. Its participants range from the Apostolic Fathers in the second century such as Ignatius of Antioch and Polycarp of Smyrna to Thomas Merton and Richard Foster in the twentieth. However, the chief concern of these writings, which have been called devotional classics, is not general or philosophical knowledge, but the articulation of ways of applying the great truths of Scripture in Christian experience and practice.

Familiarity with devotional classics, with some of the very best of spiritual reading, is valuable for two key reasons: *First* of all, it is important for all Christian believers to become acquainted with the broad spiritual history of the church which includes writers from Roman Catholicism, Eastern Orthodoxy, and Protestantism. Such familiarity is helpful in that it can undermine and actually prevent an overly provincial outlook from taking root, an outlook which could, if left uninformed, devolve into narrow readings of Scripture and into an ethnocentrism which departs from the universal love of God in Jesus Christ. And though we may not agree with all the teachings of another Christian tradition, we should at the very least acknowledge the sincerity of such Christian faith — the very same thing we expect for ourselves — and thereby open ourselves up to the possibility of learning and profiting from traditions other than our own.

Second, many of these devotional classics are very focused. For the most part, they are not concerned with highly abstract or irrelevant issues, but with the ongoing task of living the Christian life in faithfulness and with integrity. In one sense, these works are nothing less than the lab journals of the saints; their pages reflect the findings of holy men and women with respect to the "science" of the heart. They record the practices which were undertaken in the service of God and the paths which were chosen, as well as those which were not. Indeed, reading such pieces as Benedict's *Rule for Monasteries* or Luther's *Galatians Commentary* will feed the soul, refresh the spirit, and enrich our spiritual walk.

To this larger end of edification, of building up the believer, the following selections are offered as a part of a broad-based spiritual reading program. Please note that these selections which follow are not, for the most part, difficult and can be read at a leisurely pace, perhaps three or four a year. Moreover, the order in which they are read is not all that important with the notable exception that the Scriptures should be read first. In terms of the other writings, my own preference is always to read in chronological sequence. This way I can be attentive to the issues of development and change. At any rate, just find a discipline which works for you and stick with it. The selections are as follows:

1. The Old Testament
2. The New Testament
3. St. Basil the Great, *The Long Rules*
4. St. Athanasius, *The Life of Saint Anthony*
5. St. Augustine, *The Confessions of St. Augustine*
6. Benedict of Nursia, *Rules for Monasteries*
7. John Climacus, *The Ladder of Divine Ascent*
8. St. Anselm of Canterbury, *The Prayers and Meditations of St. Anselm*
9. Bernard of Clairvaux, *On Loving God*
10. St. Bonaventura, *The Mind's Road to God*
11. Author Unknown, *The Little Flowers of St. Francis*
12. Author Unknown, *Theologia Germanica*
13. Walter Hilton, *The Ladder of Perfection*
14. Thomas à Kempis, *The Imitation of Christ*
15. Martin Luther, *Galatians Commentary* (1535 edition)
16. Thomas Cranmer, *Homilies*
17. John Calvin, *Institutes of the Christian Religion*
18. St. Ignatius Loyola, *The Spiritual Exercises of Ignatius Loyola*
19. St. John of the Cross, *Dark Night of the Soul*
20. St. Teresa of Ávila, *Interior Castle*
21. Johann Arndt, *True Christianity*
22. St. Francis de Sales, *Introduction to the Devout Life*
23. Jeremy Taylor, *The Rule and Exercises of Holy Living and Holy Dying*
24. Blaise Pascal, *Pensées*
25. Philipp Jacob Spener, *Pia Desideria*
26. Brother Lawrence, *The Practice of the Presence of God*
27. William Law, *A Serious Call to a Devout and Holy Life*
28. Jonathan Edwards, *A Treatise Concerning Religious Affections*
29. John Wesley, *The Fifty-Two Standard Sermons*

30. William Wilberforce, *Real Christianity*
31. Phoebe Palmer, *The Way of Holiness*
32. Sören Kierkegaard, *Purity of Heart Is to Will One Thing*
33. Jean Caussade, *Self-Abandonment to Divine Providence*
34. Hannah Whitall Smith, *The Christian's Secret of a Happy Life*
35. Author Unknown, *The Way of the Pilgrim*
36. St. Thérèse of Lisieux, *The Story of a Soul*
37. G.K. Chesterton, *St. Francis of Assisi*
38. D. Elton Trueblood, *The Essence of Spiritual Religion*
39. Dietrich Bonhoeffer, *The Cost of Discipleship*
40. Emil Brunner, *Truth as Encounter*
41. Simone Weil, *Waiting for God*
42. Thomas Merton, *New Seeds of Contemplation*
43. Dag Hammarskjöld, *Markings*
44. Henri Nouwen, *Invitation to Life in the Spirit*

Although this list is quite broad and includes selections from many different traditions, it is by no means exhaustive. Consequently, some may take exception to the composition of the reading plan in terms of what is both excluded, *The Cloud of Unknowing*, for instance, and what is included. However, each of these works was chosen with an eye to its readability, its enduring value, and its development of the larger theme of this present work. In short, the purpose of this reading plan is to expose today's reader to a precious, though neglected, legacy. Other selections can be included as one sees fit.

Prayer

The *third* spiritual discipline which should grow out of our reading of both Scripture and devotional classics is prayer. To underscore its necessity let's think about it in comparison to that great American obsession, dieting. One of the well-kept secrets about most of the popular diets on the market today is that they don't work. The cycle is fairly typical: people go on these diets for a period of time, they lose weight, go off the diet, and then gain back all the weight they lost—and then some. And as someone who lost over 100 pounds in about a year (and kept it off) I should note that the problem is not with these diets at all, but with the attitudes that we bring to them. In other words, we should never go on a diet with the idea of going off it once the weight is lost. This is a prescription for failure. What inevitably happens is that we slowly drift back into our old, non-dieting eating habits. The key to success, then, is to change our attitude, that is, to alter our eating habits not for a couple of weeks but for life. Soon the new way of eating will not seem like a diet at all; it will *become* our normal eating pattern, and as such, it will satisfy.

In a similar fashion, if the freedom of the kingdom of God is to be continually enjoyed, if we do not wish to fall back into the kingdom of self with its old sinful patterns and behaviors, then a change in attitude, practices, and habits will be required. In particular, we must develop and maintain spiritual disciplines, especially the practice of prayer, which will then become a part of a new pattern of life — a pattern which will never end. Accordingly, one does not embark upon the Christian life thinking that all that is required is conversion and a few good intentions, for there is, after all, a life yet to be lived. Unfortunately, some Christians treat conversion like dieters treat their diets; it's all over after a few weeks. But since some of the newly awakened fail to develop a pattern of life which is open to the ongoing reception of the grace of God, they are courting spiritual disaster, and they may quickly slip back into their old sinful ways.

To be sure, when one reads the biographies of some of the most godly leaders in the church, whether it be the biography of St. Benedict of Nursia, Teresa of Ávila, Martin Luther, John Calvin, John Wesley, or Francis de Sales, a common factor quickly emerges: they were all men and women of prayer. They knew, if our modern age has forgotten it, that prayer is a remarkable vehicle for communion with God. It is a medium through which we not only reveal the deepest recesses of our hearts to God, in all honesty and humility, but through which the Most High is also graciously manifested to us. Beyond this, the Holy Spirit, present in prayer, fortifies us and enables us to live the life to which we are called. We never have to live merely out of our own strength again. Prayer connects us with the Almighty: His power becomes our power; His grace becomes our grace.

With all these positive aspects of prayer, it is truly a wonder why more Christians do not pray on a regular basis. Personal and family devotions have fallen by the wayside for some, and corporate prayer on Sunday mornings seems to be about as far as it goes for many Christians — unless, of course, some crisis erupts. But what is prayer, but the enactment, the actualization of faith. Prayer is faith reaching out beyond itself to trust and love the Holy One. Prayer is faith moving beyond temporal things to grasp the eternal. "For me," St. Thérèse of Lisieux writes, "prayer means launching out of the heart toward God; a cry of grateful love from the crest of joy or the trough of despair: it is a vast, supernatural force that opens out my heart, and binds me close to Jesus."[5]

Though not fully appreciated, there is perhaps no better indicator of the nature of one's spiritual life than this godly practice. Consequently, a Christian who never or seldom prays is like a husband who says that he loves his wife, but never wishes to speak with her. "Souls without prayer," Teresa of Ávila writes, "are like people whose bodies or limbs are paralyzed: they possess feet and hands but they cannot control them."[6] However, if this means of grace is obviously so important, then why don't Christians pray more often than they do? A number of explanations can be offered.

Obstacles to Prayer

First of all, when we embark on our spiritual journey many of us quite simply do not know how to pray. Although we can recite the Lord's Prayer, and even reflect on the words for awhile, we quickly become bored; we feel that nothing is happening. The difficulty here, and it is a common one, is that we are attempting to make prayer merely a mental exercise. That is, we attempt to pray solely with our minds, with our intellects, the very same faculties we use to prepare budgets, calculate equations, or plan vacations. However, in order for prayer to be deeply satisfying, a true encounter with God, we must learn to pray not merely with our intellect, but with our whole being: heart, emotions, imagination, *and* mind.

A second problem flows from the first. Because we live in a highly industrialized, scientific, technological culture, we are often reluctant to give free play to our imagination, especially in prayer. We somehow feel that this human faculty is not trustworthy or worse yet will lead us into grave error. But, once again, the testimony of the saints throughout the ages is quite the contrary. For example, in her own prayer life, Teresa of Ávila had the wisdom and courage to imagine her soul to be a castle with seven rooms and the seventh room, the most important of all, was at the very center of things. Each move to a different room for Teresa marked progress in her prayer life as she grew closer to God. Imagine the anticipation and excitement of Teresa as she was about to enter the seventh room and meet the King! We too can experience such wonder and joy. But we must use our imaginations; we must engage the affective levels of our being.

Or take the case of Thérèse of Lisieux who creatively used an image from nature as an aid to prayer and to understand the place of her own soul in the sight of God. In her autobiography, *The Story of a Soul,* she explains:

> But Jesus has been gracious enough to teach me a lesson about this mystery, simply by holding up to my eyes the book of nature. I realized, then, that all the flowers he has made are beautiful; the rose in its glory, the lily in its whiteness, don't rob the tiny violet of its sweet smell, or the daisy of its charming simplicity. I saw that if all these lesser blooms wanted to be roses instead, nature would lose the gaiety of her springtide dress—there would be no little flowers to make a pattern over the countryside. And so it is with the world of souls, which is his garden. He wanted to have great Saints, to be his lilies and roses, but he has made lesser Saints as well; and these lesser ones must be content to rank as daisies and violets, lying at his feet and giving pleasure to his eye like that.[7]

The image of being a flower lying at the feet of the Lord, humbly giving pleasure to His eye, was a powerful and beautiful one for Thérèse: it provided orientation toward the holy; it engaged her heart at a deep level; and it was an inducement to love.

We should, of course, feel quite free to choose our own images. Perhaps we can imagine ourselves at the cross of Christ hearing the taunts of the religious leaders and the soldiers as Jesus offered all that He had for the sake of love. And we can marvel at the strength of that love that cannot be consumed by the fires of taunting or hatred. Or perhaps we can imagine ourselves before the throne of God and all the host of heaven are falling down and worshiping the Lamb saying: "Worthy is the Lamb, who was slain, to receive power and wealth and wisdom and strength and honor and glory and praise!" (Rev. 5:12) Deeply moved, we ourselves begin to add to their voice in adoration and worship. Here the entire person is praying; the intellect — though still very much a part of things — is no longer dominant. Consequently, God is no longer merely an *object* of our thoughts; instead, He has creatively become the subject, and He begins to address us and move us at the deepest levels of our being. Meaningful prayer is like that.

Third, sometimes we have difficulty praying because we hold on to the very things which alienate us from God. For instance, how can we expect to cultivate a significant relationship with our Heavenly Father if our hearts are embittered, hardened by a lack of forgiveness toward our neighbor? Or how can we hear God's voice when we are disturbed and agitated, angry at everyone but ourselves. Or how can we appreciate the wonder and serenity of prayer if we are filled with resentment toward others or perhaps even toward God. I know a man, for instance, who was deeply troubled over his lack of attention during prayer. His once good prayer life was now in a shambles, and he couldn't understand why. After many conversations about this problem, the young man finally revealed to me that he was, in fact, resentful toward God because as he put it, "God had allowed a grave injustice to be done to me." In this case, anger and resentment, these turbulent passions, snuffed out any chance for meaningful communion.

In a similar fashion, the refusal to let go of deliberate sin will also cloud our prayer life. Indeed, if our conscience continually speaks judgment against us, if it accuses and convicts us, if it fosters anxiety, we certainly will not want to be in the presence of God. Simply put, guilt and shame will bar the way. They will become like "fiery angels" which block the path to the tree of life. The prescription here, of course, is that the offense must first be removed through the grace of God. Whether it be sexual impurity, dishonesty, greed, slander of our neighbors, hatred and jealousy of others, or any other rebellion against love, it must be eliminated. If not, the flame of God's holy love will not warm us, but will actually consume us. As St. Alphonsus Liguori once wrote: "He who does not give up prayer cannot possibly continue to offend God habitually. Either he will give up prayer, or he will stop sinning."[8]

The Stages of Prayer

As we pray, the soul usually goes through five phases: confession, adoration, intercession, petition, and thanksgiving. And though some authors place the practice of adoration first, it makes much more sense that the first thing we should do in the presence of God is to humble ourselves and confess our shortcomings. It is only then that we may proceed to adoration in the proper spirit. Continuing this line of thought, after giving due honor and praise to God, we should, of course, be mindful of others: of our friends and acquaintances who are suffering or are in need. Indeed, only when we have considered the needs of others, through intercessory prayer, may we then bring our own concerns to God in the form of petitions. And finally, we should give thanks to God for past prayer answered, the graces presently enjoyed, as well as for our hope in Jesus Christ.

Though a consideration of each major phase of prayer is beyond the scope of this book, it is important at least to consider the aspect of petition in greater detail because not only has more prayer gone awry in this area than perhaps in any other, but the solution of this problem is pertinent to our larger theme as well. The question, of course, which must be addressed is what should be the appropriate nature and content of our petitions. For what — in other words — should we pray?

When Jesus prayed in the Garden of Gethsemane, shortly before His crucifixion and death, notice that there were two aspects to His prayer. Knowing the suffering which lay ahead, Jesus prayed for another way, if it were possible: "Father, if you are willing, take this cup from me" (Luke 22:42). On the other hand, Jesus also prayed not that His own will be done but that of the

Father: "yet not my will, but yours be done" (Luke 22:42). Like Jesus, then, we too may bring all our petitions before the Father who loves and cares for us, and we are free, of course, to wrestle in prayer to attain the desires of our heart. However, when we pray, we should also, as Jesus did, place all our petitions under the greater providence, care, and will of God.

For some people, however, prayer reflects not the balance of Jesus, but it is often some obvious attempt to change God's will one way or another. It seldom, in other words, involves an active, purposeful, and obedient submission to the will of God. However, such a view (which by the way is much more common than you would think) is actually a prescription for disappointment, for it starts out wrong by pitting our own will against God's, and it then views prayer, strange as it may seem, as our successful struggle against the will of God. But should prayer really be our attempt to change God's will? If so, why should this be? Is our will perhaps better, more wise, more encompassing in its perspective? Is God's will somehow lacking, deficient in goodness or care? Again, must the Holy One be prodded to do the good which we can see but which He can't? Does the Almighty need guidance and instruction from His sinful creatures? In contrast to this anxious approach, Jesus instructed His followers not to worry about such matters as what they shall eat or drink because "the pagans run after all these things, and your heavenly Father knows that you need them" (Matt. 6:32). Instead, Jesus counseled His followers to shift their priorities, to make an about-face, in prayer: "seek first *his* kingdom and his righteousness, and all these things will be given to you as well" (Matt. 6:33).

And yet prayer is truly wrestling, but not as some suppose. It entails wrestling not so much against God, but against our own self-centered, narrow desires; it involves wrestling against our idolatry in the form of elevating penultimate things to ultimate status, in preferring the temporal and material over the eternal. Again, prayer is wrestling against privileging our own will to that of God or to that of our neighbor. In a real sense, then, we have it all backward. God is not reluctant to shower His blessings upon us as some would suppose. The problem is, however, that we have been asking for and holding on tightly to what are mere baubles, trinkets, when God wants to give us true riches. Consequently, we must first let go of our own desires in order to receive the greater gifts of God. And above all, we must not become selfish in our prayers, for this would only make a poison out of a cure.

What then should be the content of our petitions? We should pray, as Jesus Christ taught us, that the will of God may be done on earth as it is in heaven, and more particularly, that it be done in our own lives. That is, we should ever seek God's kingdom and His righteousness. This means, of course, that we are not to seek honor or praise or worldly success or any other such self-indulgent thing. Instead, we should desire love, joy, peace, patience, kindness, gentleness, self-control, even the Holy Spirit of God reigning in our hearts. Again, we should seek these good gifts, not because God is reluctant to give, but because we have been sinfully reluctant, in the past, to receive them. In short, the problem is that we have preferred our own wills to that of God's. When we pray, then, we should pray in a new and rewarding way as Jean Eudes, a seventeenth-century French pastor, wisely advised.

> Lift up your heart to him, at the beginning of every action, somewhat like this: "O Jesus, with all my power I renounce myself, my own mind, my own will, and my self-love, and I give myself all to Thee and to thy Holy Spirit and Thy divine love. Draw me out of myself and direct me in this action according to Thy holy will."[9]

But what of the trial of unanswered prayer, especially when that prayer sought the good of others? What about when we pray for our loved ones who are sick or dying, and they find no relief? Samuel Chadwick, in his book *The Path of Prayer*, describes an incident in his own life which pointedly raises this issue.

> While I was yet a young minister, one of the workers of the Church was stricken with disease. We claimed the promises, and some of the best people I have ever known prayed earnestly and believingly for his recovery. We refused to believe that faith could fail. He died while we prayed.[10]

In a situation such as this, when we have been faithful in our prayers for the good of others, and God has, for whatever reason, not answered those prayers according to our wishes, then we must humbly accept His sovereign will, believing that love is ever seeking a far greater purpose than we can understand. Clearly, it would be the height of folly and arrogance in this matter to rush into the judgment seat and to call God into question. Remember Job! Viewed another way, the cross of "unanswered" prayer is an invitation to both humility and trust. It reminds us that in life, as in death, we are not in control. And though God's circumstantial will can, in fact, be frustrated by human freedom and sin, His ultimate will which is goodness and love can never be frustrated.[11] The Lord is ever working out a far greater design than we could have ever imagined. Our task is to trust — even when it hurts.

Fasting

When many Protestants hear the word "fasting," the fourth personal discipline, they often conjure up images of a dour asceticism drawn from the Middle Ages. They envision a medieval monk in his cowl shuffling down a dark and dank church, emaciated through the rigors of fasting. Or they may associate fasting with a worn-out penitential discipline that is no longer relevant to the contemporary world. These images explain in some measure the virtual neglect of fasting as a spiritual discipline in some corners of the church. Indeed, according to one author, from 1861 to 1954 there was not a single book published on the topic of fasting in the United States![12] This amazing statistic gives ample testimony to the role of fasting in recent church history.

The neglect of this valuable means of grace is all the more troubling when we consider that the leading figures of the Bible, people such as Moses, David, King Jehoshaphat, Jesus, and Paul all fasted. In fact, there is evidence in the Scriptures which suggests that Jesus fasted on a regular basis since a novice could hardly undertake the kind of fast (forty days and nights) which Jesus did. But not only did the Messiah engage in the practice of fasting, He also taught others to do so and counseled them on the proper way it is to be done.

> When you fast, do not look somber as the hypocrites do, for they disfigure their faces to show men they are fasting. I tell you the truth, they have received their reward in full. But when you fast, put oil on your head and wash your face, so that it will not be obvious to men that you are fasting, but only to your Father, who is unseen; and your Father, who sees what is done in secret, will reward you (Matt. 6:17-18).

In light of the preceding passage, it is evident that Jesus realized that even a spiritual discipline such as fasting could become the fuel for pride and self-absorption. He, therefore, cautioned his followers that their motivation should not be self-glory, the kind of glory which basks in the attention of others; instead their motivation as well as their intent should ever be to aim at the honor and glory of God. But as long as this precaution was taken, Jesus assumed that His followers would fast as indicated by His words, "when you fast. . . ."[13]

And yet some Christians remain unconvinced. They maintain that fasting belongs to the Old Covenant not to the New, that the disciples themselves did not fast, and that Jesus approved of all this by stating that you cannot put "new wine into old wineskins." And this judgment is supposedly sustained by Matthew's account.

> Then John's disciples came and asked him, "How is it that we and the Pharisees fast, but your disciples do not fast?" Jesus answered, "How can the guests of the bridegroom mourn while he is with them? The time will come when the bridegroom will be taken from them; then they will fast. "No one sews a patch of unshrunk cloth on an old garment, for the patch will pull away from the garment, making the tear worse. Neither do men pour new wine into old wineskins. If they do, the skins will burst, the wine will run out and the wineskins will be ruined. No, they pour new wine into new wineskins, and both are preserved" (Matt. 9:14-17).

But notice that Jesus did not renounce the practice of fasting, as is mistakenly supposed. He said there will come a time, "when the bridegroom will be taken from them," that His disciples will fast. And this important truth of the *Christian* practice of fasting is borne out in the activity of the early church, as recorded in the Acts of the Apostles (13:1-3), where Paul, Barnabas, Simeon, Lucius of Cyrene, Manaen, and others all fasted after the ascension of Christ, after, in other words, the bridegroom had left — just as Jesus said they would.

Why, then, is fasting so important as a personal discipline? First of all, it helps us to focus on God in a special way. By quieting the appetite, by saying no to bodily desire, we prepare our hearts, minds, and souls to become more sensitive to the leading of God. Fasting helps us, to use the language of Brother Lawrence, "to practice the presence of God" and to be sensitive to His "still, small voice." Second, fasting is one of the natural outgrowths of serious prayer. In a real sense, fasting is the reflection of the praying heart; it makes concrete the soul's longing for the fullness of God; it says, in effect, that we are so serious and earnest in our response to grace, that we desire God above all things. Consequently, in conjunction with the other personal disciplines such as reading the Bible, studying devotional classics, and praying, fasting helps us to realize more of the beauty and richness of the spiritual life. Simply put, in denying the self, in being attentive to the One who is beyond us, fasting allows for nothing less than the possibility of God.

SUMMING UP

In this chapter we have explored the "personal" disciplines of the liberated life: reading the Bible, studying the classics of spirituality, praying, and fasting. Moreover, we pointed out that these means of grace, vital in so many ways, are necessary in order to grow spiritually. Indeed, to expect significant growth apart from their use is clearly misguided.

In the next chapter we will continue our discussion of the disciplines of the liberated life, but this time we will focus on the "corporate" and "public" disciplines: namely, receiving the Lord's Supper, participation in small groups (such as Bible studies), preparing for service in the form of self-denial, and meeting the material and spiritual needs of others.

INDIVIDUAL OR GROUP REFLECTION QUESTIONS

1 The words "liberty," "freedom," and "liberation" are often used in modern culture. Is there any difference between the contemporary meanings of these terms and their biblical usage? If so, clearly identify the differences and draw out the larger implications, especially as they relate to the ongoing Christian life.

2 Bracketing out the whole question of hermitical monks for a moment (those monks who worship God in solitude and prayer), is it possible or even desirable for the *average* Christian to live a godly life alone, apart from the community of faith? If so, how is this so? If not, why is this not the case? What would you say to a person who says that she is a Christian because she reads the Bible on a regular basis, even though she is not a part of any fellowship?

3 Distinguish prayer from each of the following: (a) thought, (b) meditation, and (c) reflection. In what ways is prayer similar to each of these activities? In what ways is it different? What are the graces and fruit of the Spirit that the practice of prayer is most likely to improve. How can prayer become a daily discipline?

EIGHT

ABIDING IN THE KINGDOM OF GOD:
The Disciplines of the Liberated Life, Part II

How I wish your bearing and conversation were such that, on seeing or hearing you, people would say: this man reads the life of Jesus Christ" (Venerable José Escriva).

Although the personal disciplines enumerated in chapter 7 are necessary ingredients to a vital Christian life, they are not sufficient by themselves and must, therefore, be supplemented by two broader sets of practices: corporate and public disciplines. The corporate disciplines, include such elements as worship, receiving the Lord's Supper, and small group activity. And though these disciplines embrace some of the very same practices of the personal disciplines such as prayer and Scripture reading, their context is markedly different. With the corporate disciplines, for example, we have now moved from the individual to the group, from the person to the community. This transition is quite natural since the church is not an assemblage of individuals, but is the body of Christ, the community of faith. The public disciplines, on the other hand, explore the even broader relation of the church to the world, of the believer to the nonbeliever.

Worship
The basic Old Testament word for worship is *abodah*, from the Hebrew *abad* which means to labor or serve. Moreover, when a

specific act of worship is referred to in the Old Covenant the word commonly used is *hishtahawah,* derived from *shaha* which means to bow or to prostrate oneself.[1] As such, Hebrew worship entailed the service of God by the people and more particularly by the priests. In time, as Alan Richardson points out, a tension developed between the priests who emphasized the traditional, ceremonial aspects of worship and the prophets like Jeremiah who highlighted the spiritual dimensions of the service of God. And although this tension must not be overdrawn, it was, nevertheless, quite real.

In a similar fashion, the basic New Testament word for worship is *latreia,* a term which also translates as the service of God, that is, divine worship. Furthermore, corresponding to the Hebrew term *hishtahawah* is the New Testament word *proskuneo* which means "to prostrate oneself, to adore, to worship."[2] And though these similarities between the two covenants in their conceptions of worship are truly noteworthy, it is even more remarkable that the same tension between ceremonial aspects of worship, on the one hand, and inward meaning and purpose, on the other, is not only duplicated in the pages of the New Testament but also intensified. Richardson elaborates:

> Jesus adopts the prophetic conception of worship, and gives the inward spiritual element absolute primacy. He does not so much attack ceremonial worship as simply ignore it. The true service (worship) of God is adoring and obedient love to him, together with loving service of one's neighbour as God's child. "This do, and thou shalt live." (Luke 10:25ff.)[3]

Richardson's point, no doubt derived from a careful reading of the gospels, is that they who worship God must do so in spirit and in truth.

On the contemporary scene, we often encounter two extreme views of worship which raise this same issue repeatedly. The one sees worship chiefly as ceremony, ritual, or performance: polished choirs, chiming bells, colorful processions, and tightly structured orders of worship are the mainstays. However, for all its refinement, this kind of service often does not enter into the deeper, richer meanings of adoration simply because it is, for the most part, impersonal and it therefore runs the risk of becoming superficial. Here ritual and ceremony can take on a life of their own, with the result that worshipers are often tempted to become mere spectators instead of participants. As D. James Kennedy, pastor of Coral Ridge Presbyterian Church and author of *Evangelism Explosion,* once quipped:

> Most people think of the church as a drama with the minister as the chief actor, God as the prompter, and the laity as the critic. What is actually the case is that the congregation is the chief actor, the minister is the prompter, and God is the critic.[4]

On the other hand, there are congregations that are so concerned about avoiding "dead formalism" that they go to the other extreme. Here singing, personal testimony, and praise constitute the entirety of worship. In a real sense, this kind of service is the camp meeting come to town—and with all its "jump and stir." In such a setting, however, you will seldom hear the Apostles' or Nicene Creed; there will be no introit or collect to give one a sense of orientation; and sometimes even the public reading of Scripture will be neglected. In fact, in such services there is little to suggest that the universal church has existed for about 2,000 years prior to these particular congregations or that the ancient church has made some vital contributions to public worship which should be heeded.

In order to rectify this particular problem, then, when we worship we should humbly and gratefully be mindful that we are a part of a much larger communion than our own individual congregations, that the body of Christ is composed not only of different denominations, but also of those numerous Christians who have preceded us. The church militant, in other words, should be mindful of the church triumphant.

In light of these two extremes, there are some simple things which we can do to make worship a more meaningful, real encounter with God which can nourish our spiritual lives. First of all, we should recognize that worship is not a matter of human initiative, but is a *response* to the grace and goodness of God. In the Old Covenant, for example, the Hebrew people did not receive many of the practices which constituted their regular worship until after they had been delivered from Egyptian bondage. More to the point, it was only after Yahweh had defeated Pharaoh through numerous plagues and in a mighty display of power that Moses and the twelve tribes then began to construct the tabernacle in the Sinai desert. Worship, in this setting, was a grateful response to the *prior* redeeming activity of God; ritual, in other words, grew out of prior deliverance.

In a similar fashion, under the New Covenant, the Christian community celebrates and worships because God has already acted and continues to act through the life, ministry, death, and resurrection of Jesus Christ. We adore and praise because God has already showered us with His redeeming grace. And we give thanks because the Father has already sacrificed His only begotten Son on our behalf. With this kind of attitude in place we come to worship service not ungrateful—"I don't get anything out of it"—but prepared to feast on the rich bounty which God lays before us in both Word and sacrament. Consequently, whenever we enter a worship setting, we must be mindful of what God has accomplished. Indeed, a spirit of gratitude and praise is the principal vehicle for meaningful worship. We love because he has first loved us; we worship and adore because we truly are a redeemed people. St. Anthony the Great said it well.

> Remember with thanksgiving [the] blessings and providence of God. Thereupon, filled with this good thought, you will rejoice in spirit and . . . brimming with the feeling of good, will wholeheartedly and with all strength glorify God, giving Him from the heart praises that rise on high.[5]

Second, in one respect at least, the problems and possibilities of worship are similar to those of prayer. In particular, we must never slip into the unfortunate pattern of viewing worship simply as a passive exercise. On the contrary, real worship is an activity—a strenuous activity. It engages our hearts, imaginations, and our minds as we respond to the grace of God. It calls for deep and meaningful participation. It involves the whole person in all that we are, and in all that we will become. So then, the next time you sing a hymn like "Crown Him with Many Crowns" be creative and imagine that the entire congregation is present at the great marriage feast and all are praising Jesus Christ because "he humbled himself and became obedient to death—even death on a cross" (Phil. 2:8). Adore Jesus. Find your joy in having *Him* praised. Deliberately add your voice to the congregation. Have it blend in, lost in a great chorus of adoration.

This is not to suggest that worship should become some kind of "emotional binge." This would be a caricature of the preceding comments. Nevertheless, participatory worship is often misunderstood and criticized by those who see it merely as emotional froth and, therefore, lacking in value and substance. These critics, of course, keep themselves above all this; they, in other words, emotionally (and psychically) detach themselves from the wonder, mystery, and beauty of worship. Perhaps it is because their cogitating intellect is ever in control. At any rate, worship is not only a mental exercise, but it is also an aesthetic experience. It is more akin to the appreciation of beauty and to the discernment of love than it is to anything else.

Actually, the problem of worship is not one of moving too deeply to the level of emotions but of not moving deeply enough to the level of dispositions, the seat of our personality. To distinguish the two, we must note that emotions are indeed fickle; they are subject to whims, time, and circumstance. Dispositions, on the other hand, are not like this; they are steadied orientations toward behavior, predisposed ways of acting which constitute our character. That is, we can feel "blue" and still be trusting Jesus Christ all the while. We can feel tired and worn out, yet on a deeper level we can be strengthened and sustained by the grace of God. We can sense a personal loss profoundly and yet continue to have unshakeable hope. And though the mighty storms of life rage around us, it can yet be quiet inside. Dispositions are like that. Jonathan Edwards called them "holy affections" and John Wesley called them "holy tempers." And it is precisely here, at this level, where God would like to touch us with His love; it is precisely here, at the very center of our being, where the Holy Spirit would like to dwell. Worship is the invitation.

Receiving the Lord's Supper

When the church comes together to worship the Most High, it often celebrates the Lord's Supper, and it does all this in obedience to the command of Jesus to "do this in memory of me." For example, on the night when He was betrayed Jesus took bread and broke it and said, "This is my body, which is for you; do this in remembrance of me" (1 Cor. 11:24). In a similar fashion, after the supper was over he took the cup and said, "This cup is the new covenant in my blood; do this, whenever you drink it, in remembrance of me" (1 Cor. 11:25). By means of these elements of bread and wine, Jesus pointed to His sacrifice which lay ahead, one (as we have indicated in chapter 6) which reconciles a sinful world to a holy God. Accordingly, the Lord's Supper is not only composed of the signs of bread and wine, but it also includes a precious promise, namely, the forgiveness of sins: "This is my blood of the covenant, which is poured out for many for the forgiveness of sins" (Matt. 26:28). In short, the Lord's Supper is nothing less than the Gospel, the good news of the forgiveness of sins, the glad tidings of salvation.

But why celebrate the Lord's Supper at all? Why isn't the proclamation of the forgiveness of sins by the preacher enough? Beyond being an explicit command of Jesus, the supper makes concrete what preaching has put into words; the supper gets down to our level as physical beings; it is an accommodation to us not as disembodied spirits, not as pure intellects, but as beings who are composed of body, mind, and spirit. Therefore, we reach out and take the elements, consume them, and have them become a part of us. These signs, then, which have the promise of the Gospel behind them, quicken our imagination; they engage our faith, and they allow us to feast on the precious offering of God's only-begotten Son.

Moreover, when we commune together, as men and women, young and old, poor and non-poor, when we transcend our differences through the universal love of God, Christ is truly among us; His unifying presence of love is made real through the power of the Holy Spirit. This presence, however, though real, can only be discerned by faith. As noted earlier, Luther pointed out that faith does not make the sacrament, but faith receives the sacrament. That is, in the Lord's Supper, Christ and the promises of the Gospel are objectively present; however, we cannot discern this presence nor receive these promises, but by faith.

So then, celebrating the supper and giving thanks to God for the gift of His Son Jesus Christ is not an individual event, nor a private affair, but a corporate activity. Here the church worships as the body of Christ, as the communion of saints, ever focused on her Lord. Here the church lifts up her voice in praise and in unison, through song and prayer, as she receives the blessings and favor of God. Here the church adores her Master, the Good Shepherd, who sacrificed Himself for the sheep, and she responds in thanksgiving for the magnificent love displayed at Calvary. Here the church militant has come alive through the activity of worship and its voice now blends with the host of heaven and with the church triumphant, a voice which will resound throughout eternity.

Participation in Small Groups

Though worship and receiving the Lord's Supper are corporate disciplines which involve the entire community of faith and are immensely valuable in fortifying us to live the Christian life, there is a sense in which they can, at times, still leave us somewhat isolated from one another, only to remain on an impersonal level. For example, few contemporary orders of worship throughout Christianity, with the notable exceptions of Pentecostalism, the Holiness movement, and the black church, permit a public and deeply personal expression of faith on the part of the congregation. Indeed, whether it be a Roman Catholic or a Presbyterian or a Greek Orthodox service makes little difference. The words of the hymns, the prayers, and the "response" to the Word are all those of other people. Interestingly enough, the congregation is only permitted to use "borrowed words" to express its faith. The great danger here, of course, is that the service may devolve into worship by proxy, and its rituals may descend into sheer performance as suggested earlier. But what would it be like if some small opportunity were made at each worship service for the personal and heartfelt proclamation of what Jesus Christ has done in our lives. Would it not be appropriate and highly fitting for a person to stand up, perhaps in a time of praise and thanks-giving, and proclaim the power of Jesus Christ to deliver from the guilt and power of sin? Such prayers are the true incense of the church as they ascend to God; such prayers are the beginnings of obedience to the counsel of Jesus to worship God in spirit and in truth.

Odd as it may seem, few communions will permit such a per-sonal and public expression of faith. Since this is the case, it is imperative that small groups be established in concert with the larger church (not in opposition to it) in order to foster the devel-opment of mature Christianity and a more personal witness. This task, although formidable, is not impossible. In fact, it has been accomplished repeatedly in the past by other serious and earnest Christians. During the seventeenth century, for example, Philipp Jakob Spener rightly discerned a similar need and met it by es-tablishing *collegia pietatis* (pious societies), in which pastors and laypeople met to study the Bible together and to share their experience of faith. Eventually, these small societies of faith be-came vital cells which fed into and nourished the larger church.

In a similar fashion, during the eighteenth century, John Wes-ley saw the need for small societies within the Methodist move-ment, which was an integral part of Anglican life and practice. Drawing from models established by others, Wesley instituted the class meeting, the band meeting, and select societies for the express purpose of making accountable fellowship possible. In the class meeting, for example, after a hymn was sung and prayers were offered to God, the leader of the meeting would ask each person to give an account of their spiritual journey. After this, the leader would respond to this sharing and perhaps offer instruction and advice. The band meeting, on the other hand, though similar in some respects to the class meeting, was com-posed of more mature Christians, and the personal examinations which occurred in this advanced setting were much more rigor-ous as revealed by the following probing questions:

(1) What known sins have you committed since our last meeting?
(2) What temptations have you met with?
(3) How were you delivered?

(4) What have you thought, said, or done, of which you doubt whether it be sin or not?

(5) Have you nothing you desire to keep secret?[6]

Beyond this, the select societies represented an inner circle of the bands, and they were by and large oriented toward the perfection of love in the heart of the believer. At any rate, whether we are considering the class meeting or the bands or Wesley's select societies, each of these meetings placed a premium on personal, accountable fellowship and thereby provided the opportunity for satisfying growth in grace.

In light of these rich traditions, it is important that the newly awakened Christian become a part of a "face-to-face" fellowship. An engaging Bible study where people can come to a greater knowledge of the Word of God as they honestly share their walk in faith is an excellent example of this. To be sure, Bible studies, by their very nature, require us to be both accountable and honest. There is little opportunity for getting lost in the crowd, so to speak, which non-face-to-face worship opportunities can permit. And besides, the mutual sharing in love and concern, the attentiveness to the needs of each member of the study, as well as the glorification of Christ which emerges in this setting, make Bible studies a particularly significant means of grace for Christians young and old alike.

PUBLIC DISCIPLINES

In one respect, redemption can be described as the process of moving from the self to the community, from the isolation of unbelief to the assurance of a communally held faith, from the alienation of pride to a fellowship of love—a fellowship where men and women find meaning and purpose together in that which is beyond themselves. To be sure, the reception of the love of God manifested in Jesus Christ motivates and empowers us to share this great gift with others, not only in the church, but beyond its walls as well. Moreover, it is through the public disciplines of self-denial, service, and evangelism that the church reaches out to enter an even broader community, a hurting world, where she can offer the healing balm of salvation. Indeed, the church can never contain this love she has received, and to keep it, ironically enough, she must give it away.

Self-Denial: Preparation for Service

Though it is well-known that self-denial is a personal discipline that often takes the form of fasting, denying our will, and sacrifice, it is less known that self-denial is also a public discipline. In fact, for many authors in the area of spirituality, self-denial is presented exclusively or almost exclusively as a personal discipline. Nevertheless, this judgment poses two key problems: First of all, when self-denial is seen solely in this way, the danger of spiritual narcissism is never far behind. In other words, one may approach self-denial simply as a means for one's own spiritual advancement. In this scenario, strange as it may seem, one denies oneself precisely in order to enhance oneself — at least spiritually. But the spiritual betterment of the self is not the exclusive, explicit goal of self-denial; instead, it is an indirect, though beneficial, consequence. One denies oneself not for the good of self, but for the good of *others,* and it is this larger perspective which has often been lost.

The second danger of identifying self-denial merely as a personal discipline is that the self can become spiritually preoccupied with itself, instead of being concerned with the needs of the poor. Here an obsessive, even morbid kind of Christianity may emerge. Some ascetics, for example, in failing to see that the goal of this spiritual discipline is the glory of God and the good of others, have maintained that the contrast to spiritual life is not unbelief and alienation, as we have argued, but the flesh, defined not as the Adamic nature or original sin, as it should be, but as *physical* existence. From Simeon Stylites, who sat atop a pole for thirty-six years in the pursuit of holiness, to ascetics who flagellated themselves, or who broke their health through virtual starvation, the pages of Christian history are filled with men and women, some of them influenced greatly by neo-Platonism, who deprecated the flesh, and thereby undervalued not only physical existence, but the goodness of the created order as well. Unfortunately, here Christianity was made to appear as a very unattractive thing in sharp contrast to the practice of Jesus of Nazareth who came, as the Bible informs us, "eating and drinking" and whose prayer was ever that people might have abundant life. Again, the opposite of spirituality is not physical existence, as some ascetics maintain. The opposite of spirituality is unbelief and self-absorption. Simply put, the God who redeems (through appropriate means of grace) is the same God who creates. There is no contradiction here.

What, then, are some of the ways in which we can practice self-denial with proper balance and for the good of our neighbor? First of all, we should cut off all needless expense.[7] After we have provided for the legitimate needs of our families and have made proper provision for their future, we should give generously to the poor, maybe even as much as the remainder of our resources. As we faithfully follow the will of God, our surplus will become the wherewithal to meet our neighbor's needs. Indeed, for disciples of Jesus Christ the gauge of success is not how much we have acquired, but how much we can do without. Developing a simple lifestyle, then, unfettered by excessive concern about *things* and becoming more concerned about *people* is a worthy and realistic goal. As Jesus taught on one occasion: "Watch out! Be on your guard against all kinds of greed; a man's life does not consist in the abundance of his possessions" (Luke 12:15).

Cutting off all needless expense, becoming frugal — a trait which undoubtedly has negative connotations in consumerist North America — does not mean that we will become stingy, penny-pinching misers, but that we will eliminate all waste and thereby become more efficient, economically speaking, with the goal, of course, of doing good to others. Moreover, industry and discipline, when they are met with such frugality, will actually increase the amount of money that we have. And for some people who view money itself and not the love of money as the root of all evil this is always a problem. However, the resources which we save, which we refuse to squander on self, can soon become a blessed means to do great good: to feed the hungry, to house the homeless, to clothe the naked — in short to bring about, at least in a small way, the kingdom of God on earth.

Nevertheless, if our industriousness and frugality are not

matched by generosity, the specter of wealth will inevitably arise. Clearly, the danger of riches, a danger which can only emerge when we refuse to give to others out of our bounty, is that we may soon set our hearts on material things, the surplus we have saved, and not on the love of God and neighbor. In fact, if we indulge, feed, and thereby aggravate foolish desire by pursuing wealth for its own sake, we will not only impoverish the self, spiritually speaking, but we will also cut off one of the principal channels that God has established to shower His grace upon those in need. Again, it is our neighbor, not ourselves, who is to be the beneficiary of all our self-denial, frugality, and discipline. Self-denial, then, really is a public discipline; it is nothing less than a channel for reform, for the amelioration of the plight of the poor.

Service: The Material Needs of Others

Empowered by the grace of God, equipped through the discipline of self-denial, we are now able to express love for our neighbors by meeting, first of all, their material needs. Of course, in any successful ministry, the physical needs of our neighbor must have chronological priority. That is, these needs must be the very first things to which we attend. Providing food for the hungry, seeking employment for the jobless, and obtaining health care for the sick should be accomplished *first* before any other deficiencies are met. Indeed, it is difficult for people to receive the good news of liberation in Jesus Christ if their stomachs are empty or they don't know where they will sleep that night. And we must remember that unselfish giving to our neighbor is valuable in and of itself; it is nothing less than a demonstration of love, a manifestation of the Gospel which can be made more clear through continued service and witness.

According to Martin Luther, ministry to others is intimately related to our vocation, our sense of calling which is to be broadly understood. To be sure, it is not just the clergy who have a vocation, a calling from God, but the laity as well. In fact, God has positioned each one of us in a place where we can bring about great good and where we can truly make a difference. Our family, church, or employment settings, for example, all provide remarkable opportunities for service: from taking meals to cancer patients to visiting the elderly, from volunteering at a soup kitchen to contributing generously when asked, from offering a sympathetic ear to a fellow worker to repairing the houses of the poor, all these activities are important expressions of love. No, we will not save the world by means of any of these small acts of love (and it is arrogant and self-righteous to think that we ever could), but we can, at least, be faithful to the call of service where God has placed us.

Nevertheless, in ministering to our neighbor, we must be careful not only to "treat symptoms," but we must also seek to rectify the underlying structural causes of poverty, homelessness, drug addiction, and the other social ills which we encounter daily. Clearly, it is better to find employment for the poor than to make them dependent on the vagaries of charity or a state bureaucracy. However, it is better yet to address the social injustice which leads to unemployment in the first place. And though these problems, at times, do seem overwhelming, we can make a difference, at least in a small way, by becoming active on the community level, by becoming politically informed, and by supporting those initiatives which will better the condition of the disadvantaged. We must learn, then, the discipline of giving our time as generously as we give our money.

Evangelism: The Spiritual Needs of Others

Although ministering to the material needs of our neighbors is not only valuable in itself but also has chronological priority in terms of other forms of ministry, it nevertheless does not have what is called valuational priority. Simply put, this first ministry of meeting the physical needs of our neighbors, while important, is not as valuable as it is sometimes mistakenly made out to be. In other words, first in time does not necessarily mean first in value. True, we must provide sustenance for our neighbors as far as we are able, but they have higher-level needs which must be addressed as well, namely, deep and lasting spiritual needs. And though our own age, which has been greatly informed by scientific empiricism and philosophical materialism, has a difficult time taking account of these spiritual needs, they are nevertheless quite real.

The proper balance between physical and spiritual needs, as well as an appropriate estimation of each, is found once again in the writings of John Wesley who labored ceaselessly during the eighteenth century to better the condition of his neighbors. In his sermon entitled "On Visiting the Sick," the Methodist leader lays out what is to be done after the temporal needs of men and women have been addressed. "These little labours of love," he writes, "will pave your way to things of *greater* importance. Having shown that you have a regard for their bodies you may proceed to inquire concerning their souls."[8] Furthermore, Wesley repeats this judgment, no doubt for emphasis, but this time he clearly displays what is the goal of all ministry worthy of the name.

> While you are eyes to the blind and feet to the lame, a husband to the widow and a father to the fatherless, see that you still keep *a higher end in view,* even the saving of souls from death, and that you labour to make all you say and do subservient *to that great end.*[9]

Accordingly, when we have made the transition from the kingdom of self to the kingdom of God and have been liberated from the cruel bondages in which we were once held, we will naturally want to share this good news with others. Redeemed by faith in Christ, empowered by no one less than the Holy Spirit of God, we now know of a greater liberty than we had ever imagined. What we once thought was impossible for us, has now been accomplished by God. Where human power and effort was futile, the grace of God has triumphed. And where the doors of our prison cell had been fastened shut, they have now swung open. This is hardly the kind of liberation about which we can keep silent, especially when opportunities for ministry abound. We can, for instance, become a part of our church's visitation team and pay a call on the unchurched in our area, or we can call on the sick, as Wesley had done, or perhaps visit with those who are in prison. But whatever form our witness to Christ takes, whatever shape our evangelism manifests, it should be done in a spirit of glad sharing and thanksgiving. It should not, in other words, be done in a coercive, argumentative spirit. Our task is to plant the seed and to spread it as widely as possible. It is up to God, not us, to give it growth.

In time, as we explore many of these opportunities for witness, as we forget ourselves and minister to others, as we work with the poor and downtrodden, we will learn one of life's more important secrets: that in giving we receive, in sharing we prosper, and in sacrificing we are made whole. Out of our joy, we shall receive more joy; out of thanksgiving, more for which to be thankful.

On the other hand, when we were imprisoned in the kingdom of self, when we thought that the way to happiness was through ambition, dominance, or through serving ourselves, we actually ended up quite unhappy, the negative emotions of greed, jealousy, and hatred having dominated our souls. But now we have found a new way, a much different way, one which, apart from the grace of God, we would have never chosen for ourselves: that fulfillment comes from sacrifice, that joy emerges from suffering, that nobility arises from humility. As Jesus taught, "Whoever finds his life will lose it, and whoever loses his life for my sake will find it" (Matt. 10:39). This is truly one of the great mysteries of life, one which can nourish us in our walk with God, open us up to the world of love and our neighbor, and keep us far beyond the kingdom of self.

INDIVIDUAL OR GROUP REFLECTION QUESTIONS

1 What does it mean to worship? That is, what does this activity say about the God whom we worship, and what does it say about ourselves? Make a chart listing the qualities and characteristics of each which worship can especially highlight. After this, list as many obstacles to the spirit of worship as you can. Are there any surprises here?

2 There are many paradoxes in the spiritual life. One such paradox is that in order to prosper in love we have to give it away. Another is that we only truly find ourselves when we lose ourselves in service. In light of this, take a spiritual inventory of your gifts and graces, seek the judgment of another, and then make a commitment to one new form of service. But above all, even in this, keep in mind the good of your neighbor.

3 Discuss ways in which you (or your group) can take practical steps to minister to the poor in your area. Explore both the motivation and goals of your ministry. What will be the major elements of your service and how will they be orchestrated to glorify Jesus Christ?

POSTSCRIPT

Our journey has been a remarkable one. We started out by exploring the fundamental problem of the human condition, and then we noted, by an appeal to the Bible and church tradition, how the lack of a trusting and caring relationship with a loving God issues in all kinds of evils, the principal one, of course, being pride or some other expression of self-rule. Simply put, if God is not on the throne of our lives, then someone or something else is.

It would be a mistake, however, to conclude that the kingdom of self is simply limited to extroverted egotists or the overly ambitious — although we have explored such types in this book. A life centered on itself, or on some other penultimate thing, such as money, career or the opinion of others, can easily take many different forms. A life so constituted, for example, is as characteristic of the competitive journalist, who is unswervingly committed to getting ahead, as it is of the retiring accountant who burns with jealousy; it is as descriptive of the braggart, who bores all in his or her presence, as it is of the laconic secretary who seethes with resentment. To be sure, pride, as we have described it, must not simply be equated with some of the more vain forms of narcissism. That would be to treat it, once again, as simply a moral problem, a particular vice, and not as an extensive spiritual and relational one.

Interestingly enough, what is often called "low self-esteem" is likewise yet another form of the kingdom of self. Here the self is related to—indeed is obsessed with—a low image of self, and it, therefore, is in a self-curving orbit which it cannot break. But unlike the narcissist, the image around which the self revolves is not an inflated and unrealistic positive one, but a negative, despairing one. Here the self, in other words, is turned in on its own negative image, which it, in part, has created (and which on some level it prefers), and it, therefore, is unable to draw its identity from that which is beyond its negativism, namely, a God of love.

We continued our journey by exploring some of the geography of the kingdom of self—how dry and barren it is!—and considered how the "liberated" self is often so quickly enslaved with the allure of money, sexual gratification, pleasure, and other attempts at a will-to-power. And here, interestingly enough, we encountered significant irony: what initially started out as an attempt to enhance the self, to increase its prerogatives, actually resulted in its enslavement. The pursuit of happiness (conceived in the form of pleasure) resulted in bondage—and in some very abject forms at that.

This weakly constituted self, however, is by no means alone. Many others are playing the same game. In light of this, we explored the strife and havoc which results when those who have made their own lives the highest value in the cosmos are confronted with others who have done precisely the same thing. This, of course, as we have pointed out, is a prescription for hell. However, the pain as well as the senselessness of this conflict may be therapeutic as the self begins to realize, ever so slowly perhaps, that the very foundations on which its life is based are faulty.

Reckoning with the delusions of the self in terms of false hope and bad faith, we maintained that the way back to serenity and integrity cannot be direct—as we might initially suppose—but indirect, requiring a mediator. The self, in other words, cannot solve "the problem of the self" nor does it have the resources to overcome the lingering effects of past evil in the form of guilt, anxiety, and fear. However, Jesus Christ, as the mediator between God and humanity, the one who knew no sin, is more than able to redeem. Not only does He satisfy the demands of justice, but He also displays the universal love of God toward sinners, toward those — whether they be black or white, male or female, young or old, ignorant or educated, rich or poor — who have rebelliously put themselves in the place of God.

Seeing the love of God manifested in Jesus Christ, getting an inkling of its strength and beauty, we are moved to trust the one who is beyond us in being, holiness, and power. Living in God through faith, we find that the walls of the kingdom of self begin to topple and self-rule begins to wane. Truly, the divine love displayed in Jesus Christ brings real power, not the phony kind of empowerment championed today, that often leaves one twice a slave of self as before. To be sure, Jesus Christ brings real liberation which delivers from all that oppresses the human spirit: jealousy, hatred, greed, revenge, indifference, resentment, anger, and despair. And finally, Jesus Christ brings not the freedom of self-will or desire, but the true freedom to love God and our neighbor as ourselves. Indeed, it is in knowing this love, feeding on its strength, that we can go beyond our limited world to enter a wider, more inclusive one, to leave behind the shackles of self and to enjoy the greatest freedom of all — the freedom to love. Yes, it has been a remarkable journey.

N O T E S

Introduction
1. "In Search of the Sacred," *Newsweek*, 28 November 1994, 54.

Chapter 1
1. Calvin S. Hall, *A Primer of Freudian Psychology* (New York: Mentor, 1954), 22ff.
2. Harry Guntrip, *Psychoanalytic Theory, Therapy, and the Self* (New York: Basic, 1973), 8.
3. This observation does not deny the importance of the unconscious and the role it plays in personality, but it does suggest a more careful and critical use of this concept.
4. James Cone, *A Black Theology of Liberation* (New York: Lippincott, 1970), 136. I am dependent on Deane William Ferm, *Contemporary American Theologies* (New York: HarperCollins, 1990) which helped to orient me to the primary literature.
5. Ibid., 118.
6. Albert Cleage, *Black Christian Nationalism* (New York: William Morrow, 1972), 96, 174.
7. J. Deotis Roberts, *Liberation and Reconciliation: A Black Theology* (Philadelphia: Westminster, 1971), 20.
8. Julius Lester, "Be Ye Therefore Perfect," *Katallagate* (Winter 1974): 25–26.
9. Mary Daly, *Beyond God the Father: Towards a Philosophy of Women's Liberation* (Boston: Beacon, 1973), 56.
10. Ibid., 59.
11. Rosemary Ruether, ed., *Liberation Theology* (New York: Paulist, 1972), 13.
12. Emil Brunner, *The Christian Doctrine of Creation and Redemption* (Philadelphia: Westminster, 1952), 115.
13. Anton C. Pegis, ed., *Introduction to Saint Thomas Aquinas* (New York: Modern Library, 1948), 120.
14. Ibid., 123.
15. John Calvin, *Institutes of the Christian Religion*, 2 vols., ed. John T. McNeill (Philadelphia: Westminster, 1960), 1:245.
16. Ibid., 1:246.
17. Ibid., 1:245.
18. Jaroslav Pelikan, ed., *Luther's Works: Vol. 1, Lectures on Genesis* (St. Louis: Concordia, 1955), 147.
19. Ibid., 1:147–48.
20. Albert C. Outler, ed., *The Sermons*, 4 vols. of *The Works of John Wesley* (Nashville: Abingdon, 1984–87), 2:477.

21. Ibid., 2:402–3.

22. Ibid., 2:480–81.

23. Brunner, *Creation and Redemption*, 92.

Chapter 2

1. To my knowledge, this phrase was coined by Earl Jabay in *The Kingdom of Self* (Plainfield, N.J.: Logos, 1974). Moreover, it is important to note that what is called "low self-esteem" is also a part of the kingdom of self. Here the self is related to—indeed is obsessed with—a low image of self. Put another way, the self is turned in on its own negative image, an image which it, in part, has created, and it, therefore, seems unable to draw its identity from the love of that which is beyond the self—namely God. This means, of course, that the kingdom of self is not to be utterly equated with narcissism which is only one of its chief forms—one, however, to which I will give considerable attention in this book.

2. Robert N. Bellah, et al., *Habits of the Heart: Individualism and Commitment in American Life* (Los Angeles: Univ. of California Press, 1985), viii.

3. Robert J. Ringer, *Looking Out for #1* (New York: Funk and Wagnalls, 1977).

4. Robert J. Ringer, *Winning through Intimidation* (Los Angeles: Los Angeles Book Publishing, 1973).

5. Shad Helmstetter, *The Self-Talk Solution* (New York: Pocket, 1982).

6. Nathaniel Branden, *Honoring the Self: The Psychology of Confidence and Respect* (New York: Bantam, 1983).

7. Cf. J. Edward Carothers, *The Paralysis of Mainstream Protestant Leadership* (Nashville: Abingdon, 1990).

8. Charles Hambrick-Stowe, "Puritan Spirituality in America," in *Christian Spirituality: Post Reformation and Modern,* ed. Louis DuPré and Don E. Saliers (New York: Crossroad, 1980), 338.

9. Gordon S. Wakefield, "Spirituality," in *The Westminster Dictionary of Christian Spirituality,* ed. Gordon S. Wakefield (Philadelphia: Westminster, 1983), 361.

10. Matthew Fox, "Roots and Routes in Western Spiritual Consciousness," in *Western Spirituality: Historical Routes, Ecumenical Routes,* ed. Matthew Fox (Santa Fe, N.M.: Bear, 1981), 1.

11. David Ray Griffin, ed., *Spirituality and Society* (Albany: State Univ. of New York Press, 1988), 1.

12. Ibid., 1–2.

13. And even those who see unbelief as the essence of evil realize that pride is at the right hand of the diabolic throne, so to speak, and they are therefore greatly appreciative of Benedict's emphasis. In a real sense, from this chapter on, these "two schools" are remarkably similar in their analysis.

14. Bernard of Clairvaux, *On Loving God* (Washington, D.C.: Cistercian, 1974).

15. Susanna Winkworth, trans., *Theologia Germanica* (London: Macmillan, 1907), 48.

16. Ibid., 50.

17. Ibid., 65.

18. Ibid., 89.

19. Philipp Jacob Spener, *Pia Desideria,* trans. and ed. Theodore Tappert (Philadelphia: Fortress, 1964), 111.

20. Harold J. Grimm, *Career of the Reformer: I,* vol. 31 of *Luther's Works* (Philadelphia: Fortress, 1957), 46.

21. Calvin, *Institutes of the Christian Religion,* 1:243.

22. Ibid., 1:242–43.

23. Outler, *Sermons* in *Works of John Wesley,* 4:154.

24. Thomas Merton, *New Seeds of Contemplation* (New York: New Directions, 1962), 181.

25. Ibid., 78.

26. Reinhold Niebuhr, *Moral Man and Immoral Society* (New York: Scribners, 1960), xx.

27. Ibid., 9.

28. Ibid., 33.

29. Richard Paul, *Critical Thinking: What Every Person Needs to Survive in a Rapidly Changing World* (Rohnert Park, Calif.: Center for Critical Thinking and Moral Critique/Sonoma State Univ. Press, 1990), 153.

30. Niebuhr, *Moral Man,* 153.

Chapter 3

1. Outler, *Sermons* in *Works of John Wesley,* 1:251.

2. Ibid.

3. Ibid., 1:253.

4. Ibid., 1:252.

5. Frederick Sontag, *A Kierkegaard Handbook* (Atlanta: John Knox, 1979), 15.

6. Kevin Philipps, *The Politics of Rich and Poor* (New York: Harper, 1990), xviii.

7. Ibid., 11.

8. "Doing What Comes Naturally," *The Economist* 317 (17 November 1990): 29.

9. Ibid.

10. Ibid.

11. Ibid.

12. Ellen Melinkoff and Janet Z. Giler, "Infidelity in the 80s: The Steamy Facts," *Cosmopolitan,* November 1988, 226.

13. Ibid., 228.

14. Richard N. Ostling, "Bishop Spong on Right and Wrong: An Iconoclastic Clergyman Fuels a Debate on Sex," *Time,* 13 June 1988, 56.

15. Ibid., 56.

16. Ibid.

17. This is not to deny that one may be a homosexual in orientation (you simply are attracted to men or women) and a child of God as well—so long as one is not dominated by lust and so long as one remains chaste. Again, all sexual intercourse, homosexual and heterosexual, outside the marriage bond is condemned in Scripture.

18. Cf. Uta Ranke-Heinemann, *Eunuchs for the Kingdom of Heaven: Women, Sexuality and the Catholic Church* (New York: Doubleday, 1991).

19. Dennis Wholey, *The Courage to Change* (Boston: Houghton Mifflin, 1984), 19.

20. Ibid., 24.

21. Gerald G. May, *Addiction and Grace* (New York: Harper and Row, 1988), 38.

Chapter 4

1. William Shakespeare, *Macbeth*, V, v, 17.

2. A remark attributed to the Englishman Sir Thomas More.

3. W.E. Sangster, *He Is Able* (Grand Rapids: Zondervan/Francis Asbury, 1988), 72.

4. Ibid., 71.

5. W.E. Sangster, *The Secret of Radiant Life* (Nashville: Abingdon, 1957), 121.

6. Cf. Jabay, *The Kingdom of Self*, previously cited.

7. Jean H. Faurot, "The Sermons of John Tauler," in *Christian Spirituality*, ed. Frank N. Magill and Ian P. McGreal (San Francisco: Harper and Row, Publishers, 1988), 167.

8. Niebuhr, *Moral Man*, xx.

9. Ibid., 9.

10. Arthur M. Schlesinger, Jr., *The Disuniting of America* (New York: W.W. Norton, 1992), 138.

11. Paul, *Critical Thinking*, 148.

12. Sangster, *Secret*, 94.

Chapter 5

1. Calvin, *Institutes of the Christian Religion*, 1:35.

2. And, of course, it must be borne in mind that young people may be at the "ethical stage" of moral and spiritual development. Moreover, these stages can overlap, at least to some extent, in a personality; they are, in other words, not as discrete as we might initially suppose.

3. Outler, *Sermons* in *Works of John Wesley*, 1:257.

4. Carl Rogers, *On Becoming a Person* (Boston: Houghton Mifflin, 1961), 37ff.

5. Emphasis is mine.

6. Immanuel Kant, *Foundations of the Metaphysics of Morals and What Is Enlightenment?* trans. Lewis White Beck (Indianapolis: Bobbs-Merrill, 1959), 85.

7. Immanuel Kant, *Critique of Practical Reason and Other Writings*, ed. Lewis White Beck (Indianapolis: Bobbs-Merrill, 1963), 146.

8. Immanuel Kant, *Religion within the Limits of Reason Alone* (New York: Harper and Row, 1960), 123.

9. Colin Brown, *Christianity and Western Thought (Volume 1)* (Downers Grove, Ill.: InterVarsity, 1990), 296.

10. Outler, *Sermons* in *Works of John Wesley*, 4:146.

11. Ibid., 1:220.

12. Emphasis is mine.

13. Felician A. Foy, ed., *Catholic Almanac* (Huntington, Ind.: Our Sunday Visitor, 1991), 222.

14. Ronald P. Patterson, ed., *The Book of Discipline of the United Methodist Church* (Nashville: The United Methodist Publishing House, 1984), 117 (par. 221).

15. Ibid., 117–18 (par. 22).

16. Emil Brunner, *The Christian Doctrine of the Church, Faith, and the Consummation* (Philadelphia: Westminster, 1962), 56.

17. Ibid.

18. Emil Brunner, *The Divine-Human Encounter* (Westport, Conn.: Greenwood, 1980), 183.

19. Outler, *Sermons* in *Works of John Wesley,* 1:428–29.

20. George Gallup, Jr. and Jim Castelli, *The People's Religion* (New York: Macmillan, 1989), 28.

21. John Naisbitt and Patricia Aburdene, *Megatrends 2000: Ten New Directions for the 1990's* (New York: William Morrow, 1990), 278.

22. Carothers, *Paralysis of Mainstream Protestant Leadership,* 69.

23. Ibid., 66.

24. Gallup and Castelli, *People's Religion,* 144.

25. Ibid., 88.

26. Naisbitt and Aburdene, *Megatrends,* 144.

27. Ibid., 277.

Chapter 6

1. Anselm, *Cur Deus Homo?* trans. Edward S. Prout (Religious Tract Society, 1880), xxi.

2. W.E. Vine, *An Expository Dictionary of New Testament Words* (Old Tappan, N.J.: Fleming H. Revell, 1940), 55–56.

3. I am indebted to John Stott for my choice of the four terms used throughout to explicate the atonement of Christ. Cf. John R.W. Stott, *The Cross of Christ* (Downers Grove, Ill.: InterVarsity, 1986), 167–203.

4. Ibid., 169.

5. Ibid., 160.

6. Vine, *Expository Dictionary,* 261.

7. Cf. Stott, *The Cross,* 192–203.

8. Wilhelm Pauck, ed., *Luther: Lectures on Romans* (Philadelphia: Westminster, 1961), 17.

9. Leon Morris, *The Apostolic Preaching of the Cross* (Grand Rapids: Eerdmans, 1955), 247.

10. Vine, *Expository Dictionary,* 263.

11. Ibid.

12. Stott, *The Cross,* 181.

13. The paragraph arrangement is mine.

Chapter 7

1. Colin Brown, ed., *The New International Dictionary of New Testament Theology*, 3 vols. (Grand Rapids: Zondervan, 1978), 3:597.

2. Vine, *Expository Dictionary*, 374.

3. St. Teresa of Avila, *Interior Castle*, trans. E. Allision Peers (New York: Doubleday, 1961), 229.

4. Karl Barth, "The Strange New World within the Bible," in *The Word of God and the Word of Man* (Gloucester, Mass.: Peter Smith, 1957), 28–50.

5. Ronda DeSola Chervin, *Quotable Saints* (Ann Arbor, Mich.: Servant, 1992), 187.

6. Jill Haak Adels, *The Wisdom of the Saints* (New York: Oxford Univ. Press, 1987), 39.

7. Thérèse of Lisieux, *Autobiography of a Saint*, trans. Ronald Knox (Glasgow: William Collins, 1958), 26.

8. Adels, *Wisdom of the Saints*, 190.

9. Ibid., 40.

10. Samuel Chadwick, *The Path of Prayer* (Fort Washington, Pa.: Christian Literature Crusade, 1956), 83.

11. I am dependent on the work of Weatherhead for the distinction between the circumstantial and the ultimate will of God. Cf. Leslie D. Weatherhead, *The Will of God* (Nashville: Abingdon, 1972).

12. Richard Foster, *Celebration of Discipline: The Path of Spiritual Growth* (New York: Harper and Row, 1978), 41.

13. Ibid., 46.

Chapter 8

1. Alan Richardson, *A Theological Word Book of the Bible* (New York: Macmillan, 1971), 287.

2. Ibid.

3. Ibid., 288.

4. Paul Lee Tan, ed., *Encyclopedia of 7700 Illustrations* (Rockville, Md.: Assurance, 1984), 1650.

5. Chervin, *Quotable Saints*, 36.

6. Albert C. Outler, ed., *John Wesley*, The Library of Protestant Thought (New York: Oxford Univ. Press, 1964), 181.

7. I am dependent on the work of John Wesley for some of the insights on this topic. Cf. Outler, *Sermons* in *Works of John Wesley*, 2:263–80.

8. Ibid., 2:391. Emphasis is mine. These hortatory comments found in the sermons reveal that in his ministry to the poor Wesley was never simply preoccupied with their temporal needs, important though they were, but he also was ever concerned with the transcendent, with the issues of God and eternity, a trait which gave his economic ethic, at least at times, a decidedly "otherworldly" emphasis. "Every pound you put into the earthly bank is sunk," Wesley writes in his "The More Excellent Way," "it brings no interest above. But every pound you give to the poor is put into the bank of heaven." Cf. Outler, *Sermons* in *Works of John Wesley*, 3:276.

9. Ibid., 3:393. Emphasis is mine.

INDEX

A

Abelard, Peter   134–35, 145
Abortion   55
Abraham   37, 88
Abstinence   68
Abuse   13, 16, 45, 100
Abyss   80
Academics   10, 37
Accountant   86, 185
Acronym   36
Activists   96
Actors   36, 170
Adam   21–24, 27, 47, 120, 142,
   150, 177
Addiction   13, 74, 76–78, 99, 100,
   102, 107, 180
Adler, Mortimer   153
Adoption   57, 102
Adoration   46, 160–61, 170, 172
Adore   48, 169, 171–72, 174
Adultery   67, 69
Advent   68
Aesthetic, (Stage)   58–59, 99, 100,
   102, 172
Affairs   69, 174
Affections   155, 172
Aging   101
Agnosticism   21, 50
AIDS   67, 150
Alcoholism   13, 74–77, 100
Alexandria, Egypt   86
Alienation   8–9, 24–25, 28–30, 32,
   65, 77, 91, 93, 95, 121, 125,
   128, 140, 144, 176–77
Altar   112
Ambition   10, 14, 27, 32, 77, 79,
   81–83, 85–86, 89, 91, 93–94,
   97–98, 182, 185
Ambrose, St.   70
Ambulance   60
America   13, 18, 62–63, 95,

116, 178
Anaxamander   153
Anaxamenes   153
Anchorites   45
Angels   55, 120, 148, 160
Anger   10, 13, 17, 77, 79, 86,
   89–93, 97, 102, 123–24, 127,
   160, 187
Anglican Church   111, 175
Anselm, St.   120, 122, 135, 145,
   155
Anthony, St.   45, 155, 171
Anti-intellectualism   38
Anti-Semitism   18
Anxiety   11, 16–17, 42, 44, 46, 58,
   68, 77, 79, 90, 115, 119, 160, 186
Apology   118
Apostles   84, 109–10, 166, 170
Appetite   37, 166
Aquinas, St. Thomas   26–27, 46
Aristotle   26
Arndt, Johann   155
Arrogance   35–36, 78, 143, 164
Art   15, 94
Ascension   166
Asceticism   86, 164, 177–78
Assisi, St. Francis   156
Athanasius, St.   155
Atheism   49
Atheists   21, 75, 105
Athletes   75, 89
Atonement   125–29, 134–35, 145
Augustine, St.   8, 25–26, 30, 46,
   48, 70, 72, 155
Authority   15, 19, 27, 83–84, 91,
   136
Autonomy   33, 49, 51, 103
Ávila, Teresa of   149, 155, 157–59
Awakening   102–3

B

Backsliding   149
Baptism   45, 85, 110–14
Barnabas   166
Barth, Karl   151
Basil, St.   155
Beauty   21, 34, 40, 47, 59, 71, 73, 166, 172, 187
Bellah, Robert   33
Benedict of Nursia   45–46, 49, 155, 157
Berkeley, University of California at   61
Bible   9, 11, 20–21, 24, 29–30, 34, 38, 48, 54, 59, 63, 68–69, 73, 83, 92, 108, 121, 125, 127, 151–53, 164, 166–67, 175–76, 178, 185
Bigotry   18
Blasphemy   136
Body   8, 25–26, 52, 56, 76, 90, 101, 111–12, 114, 120, 128, 135, 143, 168, 170, 173–74
Boesky, Ivan   61
Bonaventura, St.   155
Bonhoeffer, Dietrich   92, 156
Boredom   99, 102
Bosnia   13
Boston   19, 60–61
Bourgeoisie   21
Branden, Nathaniel   33
Bridegroom   165–66
British   49, 88
Brooklyn   108
Brunner, Emil   23, 25–26, 28–29, 113, 156
Buchanan, Tom   82
Buddhism   145
Bulimia   76

C

Caesar   136
California   61
Calvary   134, 140, 142, 174
Calvin, John   8, 27, 48, 99, 155, 157
Camus, Albert   80
Canada   89

Cancer   180
Canon   8
Canterbury, Archbishop of   120, 122, 155
Capernaum   84
Capitalism   15, 63
Career   58, 73, 101, 185
Carothers, J. Edward   38, 117–18
Carraway, Nick   82
Castle   155, 159
Catholicism, Roman   27, 49, 70, 111–12, 149, 154
Caussade, Jean   156
Celibacy   70
Cenobitic (Monasticism)   45
Chadwick, Samuel   163
Chaplain   77, 100
Charity   106, 180
Charron, Pierre   115
Cheerleader   90
Chesterton, G.K.   156
Childhood   16, 17
Christ, Jesus   10, 23–24, 38–39, 45, 47–48, 50, 52, 55, 63, 72, 83–84, 93, 106–14, 118, 120–21, 124–25, 127–36, 139–45, 147–49, 154–55, 159, 161, 166, 168, 170–76, 178–79, 181, 183, 186–87
Christianity   18, 31, 108, 114–15, 119, 145, 149, 153, 155–56, 174–75, 177
Christians   45, 63, 157–58, 165, 170, 175–76
Circumcision   113
Cistercian (Monks)   46
Clairvaux, Bernard of   46, 49, 71, 155
Cleage, Albert   18
Clergy   7, 33, 37, 117, 179
Climacus, John   155
Colossians, (Paul's letter to the)   127
Commandments   37, 64
Compassion   137, 143–44
Competition   37, 76, 78, 82, 90
Competitiveness   90, 100
Computers   78

Concupiscence 25–26
Cone, James 18
Confession 161
Confidence 33, 108, 118
Conflict 16, 39, 66, 77, 80, 89, 94, 186
Conscience 16, 33, 60, 100–101, 115, 142, 160
Conservativism 53
Consolations 80
Constantine 45
Consumers 62
Contemplation 49, 156
Contraceptive 66
Corinthians, (Paul's letter to the) 69, 72, 98, 121, 124, 128
Correctness, Political 18, 107
Cosmos 186
Counseling 10, 77, 100, 103–4, 114
Courage 49, 80, 108, 159
Covenant 132, 165, 169, 171, 173
Covetousness 64
Cranmer, Thomas 155
Creation 26, 28–29, 77
Creator 70–71, 122, 124
Creature 79, 122, 162
Crispus, Gaius Sallustius 81
Cross 8, 10, 86, 93, 120, 128, 130, 131, 134, 136–45, 149, 155, 159, 164, 172
Crucifixion 39, 136–37, 139–40, 161
Cyprian, St. 106
Cyrene, Lucius of 166

D

Death 10, 23–24, 39, 42, 44, 50, 57–58, 61, 64, 79–80, 84, 90, 99–100, 112, 117, 119, 121, 128, 133, 135–43, 148, 161, 164, 171–72, 181
Debauchery 56
Deception 36
Decius, Emperor 45
Delusions 10, 99, 101, 103, 105, 107, 109, 111, 113, 115, 117, 119, 186
Democracy 95
Demons 86, 110, 125
Denomination 40, 108, 111, 116, 170
Desires 59–60, 64–66, 72–73, 78, 108, 150, 162–63
Despair 8, 98, 100, 114–16, 118, 144, 147, 158, 187
Detroit, Michigan 62
Deuteronomy 64
Devil 28, 83–84, 86, 89, 109
Diet 156–57
Diocletian, Emperor 45
Disciples 38, 50, 84–86, 145, 165, 178
Discipleship 143–44, 149, 156
Discipline 37, 82, 111, 150, 155–56, 164–67, 177–80
Discrimination 97
Disease 14, 25, 30, 79, 163
Disobedience 22, 24, 27, 143–44
Divine 21, 29, 68, 94, 105, 107, 110, 118, 121–23, 127, 134, 139, 145, 151, 155–56, 163, 169, 187
Divorce 121
Dominican (Order) 41, 94
Domitian, Emperor 45
Dostoyevski, Fyodor 94
Doubt 17, 21–22, 27–29, 41, 50, 60, 65, 77, 86, 88–89, 109, 117, 122, 129, 133, 135, 144, 151, 169, 176, 181
Dreams 16
Drugs 78
Drunkenness 57–58, 75
Dryden, John 87
Duty 105, 109
Dylan, Bob 148

E

Earth 31, 38, 65, 70, 128, 141, 163, 178
Economics 14–15, 29, 52, 63, 95, 97
Eden, Garden of 120

Education 59, 73, 119
Edwards, Jonathan 155, 172
Egoism 51, 53, 95–96, 185
Emotions 14, 158, 172, 182
Empiricism 9, 180
Emptiness 73, 77
Enlightenment 48–49, 105
Envy 10, 30, 62–63, 77, 79, 86–89, 93, 97, 102
Equality 33, 141
Erikson, Erik 17
Eternity 58, 101, 174
Ethics 51, 105–6, 117
Ethnicity 98
Ethnocentrism 42, 96, 98, 154
Europe 15
Evangelicals 117
Evangelism 11, 170, 176, 180–81
Eve 21–24, 27–28, 120, 142
Existentialism 80

F

Faith 24–25, 28, 30, 33, 42, 45, 86, 99, 105–7, 109–14, 116, 119–20, 125–26, 129–31, 134, 141–42, 144, 147, 149–52, 158, 163, 167–68, 173–76, 181, 186–87
Faithfulness 120, 144, 154
Faithlessness 27
Falsehood 22, 28
Family 55, 61, 64, 68, 90, 158, 179
Fanaticism 110
Fantasy 58, 78, 101
Fasting 11, 151, 164–66, 177
Fear 11, 24, 44, 47, 57, 65, 86, 87, 88, 90–91, 119, 124–25, 145, 149, 186
Fellowship 76, 98, 113, 124, 142, 167, 175–76
Feminism 17, 19, 21
Feuerbach, Ludwig 49
Fitzgerald, F. Scott 82
Fixx, Jim 79
Folly 109, 164
Foolishness 118, 141
Forgiveness 122, 130–31, 133, 142, 145, 160, 173
Fornication 69
Fourteenth century 47, 94
Freedom 35, 57–58, 74, 95, 100, 112, 132, 144, 148–49, 157, 164, 167, 187
Freud, Sigmund 9, 14–17, 29, 49
Friendship 90, 128
Frugality 178–79
Frustration 74, 107
Fundamentalism 107–9

G

Galatians, (Paul's letter to the) 132, 154–55
Gallup, George 116–17
Gambling 78
Gatsby, The Great 82–83
Gender 20, 97–98
Genesis, (Book of) 21–23, 27–28, 70
Gentiles 75
Gethsemane, Garden of 161
Glory 31, 39, 48, 55, 85, 87, 122–23, 134, 141, 159–60, 165, 177
Gluttony 10, 59, 114
God 7, 9–11, 18–37, 39–40, 42–43, 45–50, 52–55, 57–60, 63–65, 68–74, 76–80, 83–84, 86–88, 91–94, 97–99, 102, 105–6, 108, 110–45, 147–83, 185–87
Goddesses 37
Godlessness 36
Godplayers 93
Golf 78
Gospel 20, 36, 38, 40, 45, 61, 64, 79, 83, 85, 108, 110, 115, 118–19, 129, 131–32, 134–37, 141, 146, 173–74, 179
Gossip 74, 78
Grace 10–11, 23–24, 34–35, 43, 48, 72, 76–78, 102, 105–6, 110–12, 114, 116, 121–22, 125, 129, 132–34, 140–42, 144–45, 149–53, 157–58, 161, 164, 166, 170–72, 176, 178–79, 181–82

Greed   10, 15, 30, 36, 57, 59, 61,
    63–64, 161, 178, 182, 187
Greeks, The   148
Guilt   11, 42, 44, 68, 79–80, 101,
    103, 112, 115–16, 119–21, 125,
    127, 129–31, 134, 138, 141–42,
    149, 160, 175, 186
Gunman   60, 90
Guttmacher, Alan   67

H

Habits   26, 33, 157
Hambrick-Stowe, Charles   41
Hammarskjöld, Dag   50–51, 156
Happiness   35, 49, 59–60, 62, 66,
    68, 74, 77, 91, 100, 144, 182,
    186
Harnack, Adolph von   106
Hatred   14, 79, 137, 139–41,
    160–61, 182, 187
Healing   16, 29, 39, 77, 93, 124,
    134, 145, 177
Health   20, 40, 150, 177, 179
Heathen   25
Heaven   38–39, 41, 55, 65, 89, 117,
    128, 141, 147, 160, 163, 174
Hebrews   69, 132–33
Hegel, Friedrich   15
Heinz, John   79
Hell   50, 77, 89, 108, 117, 186
Helmstetter, Shad   33
Hermits   45
Herpes   67
Hinduism   145
Hippies   66
Hite, Shere   67
Hoffman, Abbie   66
Holiness   24, 70, 115, 121–23, 156,
    174, 177, 187
Homelessness   59, 62–63, 178,
    180
Homosexuality   69
Honesty   10, 50, 157
Honor   36, 39, 55, 81, 85, 89,
    123–24, 160–61, 163, 165
Hope   60, 77, 93, 99, 113,
    115–16, 121, 130, 137, 144,

    161, 172, 186
Humanism   50
Humility   34–35, 38–39, 46–47, 49,
    70, 78, 127, 141, 157, 164, 182
Hymns   172, 174–75
Hypocrisy   36–37, 139–40
Hypocrites   36, 165

I

Id   16
Idealism   15
Ideology   20, 53, 130
Idolatry   27, 32, 47–49, 64–65, 162
Illinois   56
Immorality   56
Immortality   101
Independence   24, 29, 31, 49, 51,
    103, 105, 147–48
Individualism   33
Infidelity   67
Infirmities   138
Injustice   46, 50, 53, 91–92, 96,
    160, 180
Insecurity   17, 79–80, 90, 97
Integrity   10, 20, 43–44, 61, 74,
    101, 125, 129, 154, 186
Intercession   139, 161
Intercourse   67, 69
Intimacy   66, 71
Introit   170
Irenaeus   26, 141
Isaiah   42, 138
Israel   37, 46, 113, 136–37, 139

J

Jabay, Earl   10
Jazz   83
Jealousy   14, 17, 79, 88–89, 98,
    136, 139, 148, 161, 182, 185,
    187
Jehoshaphat   164
Jeremiah   169
Jerome   70
Jerusalem   39, 92, 136
Jesus   23–24, 36–41, 45, 47, 55,
    63–65, 77–78, 83–86, 92–93,

108–10, 112, 114, 118, 121,
124–25, 127–44, 147, 149, 154,
158–66, 168–69, 171–76,
178–79, 182–83, 186–87
Jews   75, 137
Jobless   179
Joy   7, 10, 49, 86–87, 92, 102, 147,
158–59, 163, 172, 182
Judea   37, 136
Justice   20, 26–27, 29, 47, 50, 52,
64, 93, 95–98, 121–23, 126, 187
Justification   63, 73, 96, 125,
129–31, 135, 138, 145, 150

K

Kant, Immanuel   41, 105–6, 130
Karamazov, The Brothers   94
Kennedy, James   170
Kentucky   50
Kierkegaard, Sören   57–58, 101–2,
119, 156
Kubler-Ross, Elizabeth   58

L

Laffer, Arthur   63
Latin   25, 70
Law   40–41, 57, 75–76, 104, 129,
132, 137, 139–40, 145, 155
Laypeople   38, 175
Laziness   114–15
Lesbianism   69
Liberalism   17, 53
Liberation   14, 19, 51, 102, 113,
119, 148–49, 167, 179, 181, 187
Liberty   39, 54, 57, 61, 76, 148,
149, 167, 181
Liguori, Alphonsus   161
Lincoln, Abraham   88
Lisieux, Thérèse De   147, 156,
158, 159
Literature   8, 15, 17, 33–34, 38, 82
Locke, John   153
Lombardi, Vince   81
Loneliness   102
Love   18, 25, 37–40, 42, 46–47, 49,
50, 52–54, 59, 65–67, 69, 71,

73, 77, 83, 87, 92–95, 114, 116,
122–26, 130–34, 136, 139–45,
147, 149, 153–54, 158–61,
163–64, 169, 171, 172–74,
176–82, 186–87
Lowliness   45, 141
Loyola, Ignatius   155
Lucius of Cyrene   166
Lust   10, 14, 19, 25, 30, 57, 59, 61,
69, 72, 104, 148
Luther, Martin   8, 27, 42, 48, 70,
97, 111, 129, 131, 154–55, 157,
173, 179
Lying   159

M

Madness   115
Mainline Churches   108,
116–18
Malnutrition   14
Manaen   166
Marriage   58, 66, 68–69, 72, 82,
172
Mars   57
Martyrdom   45
Marx, Karl   9, 14–15, 29, 31, 49,
153
Marxism   29, 63
Maslow, Abraham   46
Mass   111
Masturbation   108
Materialism   7, 58, 180
Meaninglessness   80
Media   119
Meditation   167
Memphis, Tennessee   112
Menninger, Karl   7
Mercy   106, 144
Merton, Thomas   49–50, 153, 156
Messiah   18, 131, 133, 138–41,
143, 164
Metanoia (Conversion)   121
Metaphysics   21
Methodism   28, 57, 102, 111
Michelangelo   87
Milken, Michael   61
Ministry   83, 85, 124, 136–37, 143,

171, 179, 180–81, 183
Miracles   40, 139
Monasticism   45–46, 50, 70, 134,
    154–55
Money   10, 54, 56, 59–63, 65–66,
    77–78, 80, 83, 92, 99, 178, 180,
    185–86
Monks   45, 49, 71, 86, 94, 164, 167
Monogamy   68
Monotheism   53
Morality   41–43, 66, 106
Mortality   15, 58, 101
Moses   164, 171
Music   66
Musicians   75
Mystics   46–47
Myth   17, 33, 62, 75
Mythology   22

N

Narcissism   177, 185–86
Nationalism   18
Naturalism   7, 9
Nazarene, Church of the   116
Nazareth   39, 137, 178
Negativism   186
Neoplatonism   26, 177
Nero, Emperor   45
Neuroses   16
Newsweek   8
Niebuhr, Reinhold   51–53, 95
Nietzsche, Friedrich   49, 80
Non-directive counseling   103
Nouwen, Henri   156
Nursia, Benedict of   45, 49, 155,
    157

O

O'Neill, Nena   66
Obedience   24, 29, 46, 84, 121,
    148, 173, 175
Obsession   62, 148, 156
Oedipus complex   17
Opiates   57, 102
Opium   31
Oppression   19–20, 138

Optimism   15, 107, 142
Orthodoxy   98, 107, 109, 114,
    118, 149, 154
Oxford University   28

P

Pachomius   45
Pagans   162
Palmer, Phoebe   156
Parables   39
Parenthood   67
Parents   64, 67, 82, 111
Pascal, Rene   155
Passions   123, 148, 160
Pastor   108, 111, 163, 170
Patience   16, 40, 103, 144, 163
Patriarchy   19
Peace   7, 39, 46, 68, 77, 86, 88,
    91–92, 102, 120–21, 128, 130,
    134, 138, 143, 163
Peck, M. Scott   7
Pentecostalism   174
Perfection   49, 72, 155, 176
Permissiveness   122
Persecution   45
Pessimism   142
Pharaoh   171
Pharisees   36–37, 41, 139–41, 165
Philosophy   15, 21
Pia Desideria   155
Piety   45
Planet   98
Plato   8
Pleasure   10, 16, 38, 42, 56, 58–59,
    66, 72–77, 80, 98–100, 159, 186
Pluralism   95
Poet   18, 59
Police   60–61
Politics   13, 63
Pollsters   116
Pollution   13, 129
Polycarp   153
Poor   48, 51, 53, 62–63, 75, 82,
    125, 137, 173, 177–80, 182–83
Pope Leo XIII   27
Popularity   136
Possessions   65, 178

Postmodernism 8
Poverty 14–15, 20, 31, 180
Praise 38, 40, 55, 63, 81, 134,
     160–61, 163, 170–71, 174–75
Prayer 100, 117, 147, 151,
     156–64, 166–68, 171, 174, 178
Preachers 20, 40
Preaching 15, 40, 106, 131, 173
Prejudice 18, 34, 52, 96–97
Presbyterian 116, 170, 174
Presidency 89
Presumption 98, 114–16, 118
Pride 10–11, 25, 27–28, 30–32,
     34–38, 43–44, 48, 54–55, 59,
     72, 74, 78, 98, 102, 104, 127,
     130, 134, 143–44, 149, 165,
     176, 185
Prison 132, 181
Procreation 25, 70
Prodigal Son 79
Prohibition 22
Proletariat 15
Promiscuity 17, 76
Prophets 42, 169
Propitiation 125–27
Prostitution 15, 107
Protestantism 49, 70, 154
Proverbs, (Book of) 35
Providence 156, 162, 171
Psalm 26
Psyche 20
Psychiatry 15
Psychoanalysis 16
Psychology 13, 20, 33
Psychotherapy 15

R
Rabbi 36
Racism 18–19, 31
Radicalism 17
Rage 14, 79, 172
Ransom 125, 131–33
Reagan, Ronald 62–63
Realism 52
Rebellion 17, 25, 29, 43, 69,
     121–22, 128, 130–31, 136, 145,
     150, 161

Redemption 28, 107, 111–12,
     124–25, 127, 130–34, 176
Reformation 27, 48–49, 70, 129
Regeneration 111, 145, 150
Religion 15, 17–18, 27, 31, 33, 41,
     43, 48–49, 96, 99, 105–6, 109,
     114–17, 130, 155–56
Religiosity 116
Repentance 30, 102, 121
Republican Party 53
Resentment 13, 46, 75, 89, 92, 95,
     160, 185, 187
Resolutions 103, 108
Resurrection 24, 108, 117, 144,
     171
Retirement 59
Revelation 55, 94, 134
Revenge 14, 102, 148, 187
Revolution 62, 67, 130
Richardson, Alan 169
Riches 48, 61, 63–65, 133, 163,
     179
Righteousness 40–41, 115,
     120–22, 125–27, 129–31, 134,
     145, 148, 162–63
Ringer, Robert 33
Ritschl, Albrecht 41, 106
Roberts, Deotis 18
Robinson, John A.T. 117
Rogers, Carl 62, 103
Roses 159
Rousseau, Jean Jacques 95, 106
Rubin, Jerry 66
Ruether, Rosemary R. 19
Ruysbroeck, Jan Van 47

S
Sacramentalism 110–12, 114, 118
Sacraments 110–14, 171, 173
Saducees 139–41
Saints 132, 154, 159, 174
Salvation 105, 107, 109, 112, 121,
     128, 130, 132–35, 145, 173, 177
Sanctifying (Grace) 43, 150
Sangster, W.E. 88, 98
Sanhedrin 136
Sartre, John Paul 80

Satan 27–28, 84
Savior 112, 140, 147
Schlesinger, Arthur, Jr. 95
Scholasticism 107
Science 15, 20, 29, 88, 154
Scripture 8, 24, 29, 68, 71,
 122–23, 127, 133, 147, 153–54,
 156, 168, 170
Self-will 28, 32, 36, 47, 49, 68,
 76–77, 91, 102, 130, 134, 148,
 187
Selfishness 33, 51, 53, 96
Seminary 51, 152
Serenity 74, 92, 108, 160, 186
Sex 10, 17, 29, 54, 56, 58–59,
 66–69, 77, 99
Sexism 18–19, 31
Shame 18, 81, 101, 103, 120, 140,
 141, 160
Sickness 26, 88
Simeon 166
Sin 7–8, 17–19, 21–31, 35, 37, 48,
 57–58, 65, 68, 70–72, 76, 84,
 102–4, 106, 109, 111–13, 115,
 119–25, 127–34, 139, 141–45,
 148–50, 160, 164, 175–77, 187
Sincerity 154
Slander 69, 161
Slavery 65, 73, 77, 105, 131, 148
Sloth 114–16, 118
Smith, Hannah Whitall 156
Smoking 76
Socialism 20, 63
Sociologists 51, 66–67
Sodomy 69
Soldiers 136–37, 160
Solitude 167
Solomon 71
Sontag, Frederick 59
Souls 8, 142, 158–59, 166, 181,
 182
Spener, Philip Jacob 155, 175
Spirituality 8–9, 26, 31, 34, 41–43,
 45, 49–50, 53–54, 68, 70–72,
 76–78, 96–97, 105–6, 116,
 118–19, 166, 177–78
Spong, John Shelby 68
Starvation 177

Statistics 67, 75
Steroids 90
Stott, John 127
Strife 10, 77, 79, 86, 89–91, 93, 95,
 97–98, 100, 186
Stupor 57
Stylites, Simeon 177
Submission 29, 34, 49, 78, 149,
 162
Success 59, 73, 75, 81, 83, 86–88,
 91, 147, 157, 163, 178
Suffering 35, 73, 77–78, 84,
 93–94, 97, 100, 102, 112,
 138–40, 146, 161, 182
Superego 16
Superstition 106
Syphilis 67

T

Tabernacle 171
Taboos 109
Tauler, John 94
Taylor, Jeremy 155
Tea 82
Televangelists 63
Television 32–33, 68
Temple 37, 92, 137
Temptation 8, 21–23, 65, 82–83
Tertullian 70
Thales 153
Thanksgiving 161, 171, 174–75,
 181–82
Theodosius the Great 45
Theologian 18–19, 23, 27, 41,
 46–47, 51–52, 57, 72, 95, 122,
 134, 151
Theology 18–19, 21, 25–26, 29,
 38, 119
Therapist 16, 67, 103
Therapy 16, 104
Thieves 65, 69, 114
Thoreau, Henry David 13
Tillich, Paul 41
Tobacco 78
Tocqueville, Alexis de 33
Tracts 108
Tradition 8, 28, 44, 49, 54, 70,

111, 153–54, 185
Transcendence   8, 42, 54, 106, 119
Transvaluation   147
Trappist (Monks)   49–50
Trespasses   23
Tribalism   96
Trueblood, D. Elton   156
Trust   23–25, 27, 29–30, 32, 34,
    39, 65, 71, 109, 121, 124, 133,
    158, 164, 187
Truth   7, 22, 28–29, 77–78, 86, 89,
    94, 105, 108, 131, 134, 153,
    156, 165–66, 169, 175
Twentieth century   14, 20, 23, 49
Tyranny   51, 53, 148

U

Unbelief   9–10, 23–25, 27–32, 43,
    48, 59, 72, 87, 122, 127–28,
    130, 134, 143, 149–50, 176–78
Unchurched   181
Underachievers   82
Unemployment   180
Unfaithfulness   27
Universe   93, 122–23, 143
University   61, 96
Urban   67
Utopias   118

V

Vacation   58–59, 62, 101
Values   7, 9–10, 21, 33, 38–39,
    41–42, 53–54, 78, 97, 100–101
Vanity   76
Vice   30, 38, 43–44, 82, 98, 185
Viciousness   30
Victim   20, 67
Vietnam   66
Violence   32, 138
Virginity   70, 72
Vocation   179
Vows   111

W

Wakefield, Gordon   41
Wealth   55, 60–65, 78, 81, 83, 160,
    179
Wedding   82, 109
Wesley, John   8, 28, 48–49, 57,
    102, 109, 113, 155, 157, 172,
    175, 181
Whiskey   100
Whoremongers   114
Wickedness   28, 37, 131, 142
Widow   181
Wilberforce, William   156
Will-to-power   186
Wineskins   165
Winning   33, 78, 81, 147
Wisdom   21–22, 35–36, 45, 47, 55,
    62, 64, 68, 77, 89, 99, 118, 141,
    159–60
Woman   21–22, 27–28, 74, 90, 101,
    139
Workshops   117
Worldview   29, 119
Worry   162
Worship   83–84, 106, 160, 167–76,
    182
Wrath   64, 122–23, 127, 129, 131,
    142

Y

Yahweh   20, 171
Yankee   33
Youth   59, 100–101

Z

Zebedee, Sons of   85
Zion   40
Zossima, Father   94
Zurich   113